PREPPING
FOR THE
Bookshelf

Master Planning Tips and Publishing
Strategies for Indie Authors

SHANA N. MURPH

REVISE AND REWRITE EDITORIAL
PHILADELPHIA

Copyright © 2022 Shana N. Murph

All rights reserved. No part of this book may be reproduced in any form or by any electronic or mechanical means, including information storage and retrieval systems, without permission in writing from the publisher, except by reviewers, who may quote brief passages in a review.

ISBN- 978-1-7361985-1-3 (paperback)

ISBN: 978-1-7361985-2-0 (e-book EPUB)

Library of Congress Control Number: 2021919363

www.reviseandrewrite.com

Printed in the United States of America

Published by Revise and Rewrite Editorial, LLC

Table of Contents

Introduction	1
Chapter 1 Master Planning: Creating a Book-Publishing Plan	5
Chapter 2 Book Anatomy: Building a Book from Concept to Draft	25
Chapter 3 Book Editors 101: What They Do and How They Do It	45
Chapter 4 Art, Covers, and Layout Design: Working with Designers	61
Chapter 5 Copyright Pages, Publishing Contracts, and Protecting Your Work	73
Chapter 6 The Author Brand: Your Prose Is Your Platform	85
Chapter 7 How to Develop and Grow Your Author Brand	97
Conclusion	112
References	114
Appendix A Questions to Ask Creative Professionals	118
Appendix B The Publishing Readiness Checklist	132
Appendix C Chapter Development Worksheet	136
Index	139

Introduction

There are many ways to self-publish a book. Writers of every genre can independently publish any work whether it's a short manual or pamphlet, a 200-page nonfiction title, a gripping 400-page novel or an 800- page textbook. Methods vary from writer to writer, but self-publishing can either be a painstakingly long haphazard process or a well-ordered book-producing machine. It can be an incredibly fulfilling labor of love or leave a writer drowning in frustration. Being a successful indie author hinges on how well you handle the details—the nuts and bolts of every aspect of publishing. Those details include everything from:

- Goal setting and your method for writing
- Idea sourcing
- Creating a publishing plan
- Gathering research and audience feedback
- Organizing content
- Writing chapters
- Choosing a title
- Setting the price
- Understanding quality layout and cover design
- Researching publishing platforms (print, e-book, enhanced e-book, audiobook)
- Planning your book launch.

Managing all of that without breaking a sweat is all about mastering three areas: your self-publishing plan, the development of your manuscript and the marketing of your book. How you plan for success, put pen to paper, position your book in the marketplace, and establish your author brand makes all the difference.

Are you drowning in the details?

The plan you create becomes your blueprint. Once you have created a plan, you will use that as a template for every book you publish. In your planning you will write out all the steps you need to launch your book and note all the moving parts—all while managing your budget, platform, and selling strategy. Unfortunately planning ahead sometimes takes a back seat because creating is so exciting and it's a beautiful part of the publishing process. Many can't wait to finish and begin sharing their books with the world. But if you plan ahead of time, you'll ensure that the self-publishing process also becomes a satisfying part of your writing journey. A plan prepares you for problems that pop up down the road. A high-quality book that will represent you well for years to come doesn't just happen and neither does a focused writing strategy.

As an editor and writer, I know the writing process can be both thrilling and difficult, but it is less stressful when you develop a winning writing and editing strategy. Your pen-to-paper process should also include a best practice approach including working with editors, designers and even project managers, who are essential to producing a book that will serve your audience well. If your book isn't written, organized, and edited well, it will impact your entire image—whether that's business or personal. Creating your first draft and working with creatives in the book publishing space can be a successful collaborative effort. Knowing various book development techniques and finalizing your manuscript will help you put your best foot forward and position you for a successful launch.

It's a fact. No one wants to prop up a poorly done book. You want to release a book that has checked off all the boxes. Audiences want a book that not only looks good, but reads well—a book that, is just as awesome as it's design. As every lucrative publisher knows, planning makes the writing process more focused and appealing. Just as publishers use book proposals and other methods to drive sales and increase the likelihood of success, you can adopt some of these same tried and true methods (and a few newer ones) to take the pain out of your publishing process. *Prepping for the Bookshelf: Master Planning Tips and Publishing Strategies for Indie Authors* aims to help self-published writers avoid major pitfalls that could derail their publishing goals and ruin their author brand.

CHAPTER 1

Master Planning: Creating a Book-Publishing Plan

Successful book writing begins with knowing your purpose for writing. You'll want to ask yourself, why am I writing this book? Who am I writing to? Is this book designed to help people (self help), teach people (how-to or textbook), or inspire people to act? Do I want to share my story and encourage someone (memoir, autobiography)? Am I bringing an issue or an event to light (narrative nonfiction, history)? When you know why you are writing, you can better picture your audience, and that snapshot in your mind will guide and motivate you to not only start, but to plan effectively, finish writing, and launch your book. As many can attest, it's easy to start a book, but many writers struggle to finish. When you are motivated with a clear reason, a clear objective, you will plan better and push yourself to the finish line.

The first step to ensuring you start and finish your book is creating what I call the ultimate master planning playbook. Your master plan consists of seven parts. Each part serves to not only help you finish your book, but help you publish and market a high-quality product. Master planning includes determining budget, objectives, goals, target audience, competition, publishing date, schedule, publishing platform, and drafting your marketing and advertising plan (but that is only the beginning). Let's begin with the first step.

STEP 1: SET YOUR GOALS

Objectives. There are three main reasons why people read books. They read to **learn**, they read to **solve problems**, or they read to **inspire or entertain** themselves. Will your book educate, solve a problem or inspire/entertain? Once you understand your main reason for writing, you can identify your **objectives or goals**. What do your readers want to learn? How will they use this information? What will readers do with this information?

Try picturing your reader before and after they read, and remember them as you write. Imagine their faces and picture their smiles. Post your readers problems, joys or desires near your writing spaces—on walls, on your desk, etc.

"My reader needs help with_____."

"How will my reader accomplish_____?"

"My stories give my readers_____."

Knowing your objectives and goals will guide your writing. For example, if your goal or objective is to influence or persuade people to advocate for something, you must focus on why they shouldn't hesitate. Focus on what would cause your readers to say no instead of focusing on all the many ways it's a good idea. Why should they care? A focused writing process allows you to develop content that is relevant, organized, and clear. Sometimes authors become too self-consumed. Try not to be too intent on getting every single point or idea into one book. Instead, think about the reader's needs and desires. You want to help readers, not overwhelm them. Some titles can be really detailed and comprehensive, such as biographies or textbooks, but popular books are focused on clear objectives and not laundry lists of every topic under the sun. Staying connected to your goals ensures that your content doesn't stray too far away from your purpose for writing in the first place. Another great benefit to setting goals and objectives is that it will drive your marketing strategy later.

STEP 2: NARROWING YOUR TARGET AUDIENCE

Target Audience. This is a significant part of the planning process because this gives your book a more definitive direction—a designation, the heart, head and soul of your reader. Your ideal readers will notice you right away. But not knowing your audience is like releasing your book into a black hole and hoping someone will see you in the dark. I call it publishing into the unknown abyss, where an author is wading around in an area when no one is looking or paying attention. In order to stand out so that readers can find you, you need to write to a targeted group. Writing to everyone is like writing to no one. Don't focus on a large segment of the population. Writing to a wide demographic doesn't help your book to stand out. If your content is too general, readers are less likely to find you. Your audience should be specific because books by design are specific.

Think about it this way: mass communication and book publishing are vastly different fields. With mass communication the main objective is to inform the neighborhood or country at large and tell them what's happening locally and everywhere. But book readers look for specific topics. If they stumble onto something too general or vague, it won't grab their attention, and to grab their attention, you need to tap into what they are looking for. In order to do this, you need to know your readers well. You want to know your target audience like you would know your neighbor or a close friend. You need to know age, educational background, gender, where they live, cultural background, ethnic background, musical tastes, religion, occupation, what makes them get up in the morning, etc. Be as detailed as possible. What are their problems? What do they enjoy? How many kids do they have? What is the reading level of your ideal reader? If your readers are carefree with fewer time constraints, they may enjoy a longer book. Busy readers enjoy short books. Is your reader a busy mom or are they retired with time on their hands? Are your readers visual learners? If so, your book should contain photos, illustrations, or colorful tables.

Dig further into your audience by gathering research. Look up book stats to learn certain facts, such as the most popular genres, popular topics according to age or gender. Knowing your target audience is about knowing them in a variety of ways, ways that will help you connect with them on an intimate level. Local libraries are equipped with resources to help you research general demographics and specific details about your reader's lifestyle and hobbies.

STEP 3: LEARNING THE MARKETPLACE

Competition. Considering other books similar to yours will help shape your **marketing and advertising** strategy whether you do it yourself or hire a book marketer. Assessing similar titles is key to writing and marketing a book that represents you well on a bookshelf filled with other books. Ask yourself: Are there books similar to the one I'm writing? How will my book be different from other books in my genre? What kind of value does it add in comparison to other available books? What kind of impact will it have? How will my book stand out? In order to position your book well in a sea of hundreds of books, you'll want to know what is out there and how those books compare to yours.

The most successful books fill a void. Stand out and position your book as an upgrade or a better alternative to what is out there now. To do this you don't need to read every book out there that is similar to yours, but if you are writing about a heavily covered topic, ensure your book isn't the same as everyone else's.

You don't want to be repetitive or offer a downgraded version of a better book. Another important tip to remember is that you aren't necessarily looking for other authors/editors/publishers to validate your work per se. This step is primarily about positioning your book well; it's not about validation.

Tips for Evaluating Similar Titles

Table of Contents and Index: Take a look at the book's coverage of topics. Are you covering the same information? Will you be adding more than what other books cover or less? Searching for key terms in the index will also tell you something about what is covered.

Cover Design: Notice the layout and the elements used. Did the author choose to use a photo, an abstract graphic, an illustration or, drawing? How engaging is the cover? Is it professional and well done? If the cover is well done, your cover must be just as inviting.

Writing Style: Some authors take a more formal approach to their coverage of topics, while others are more casual. Does the author write in passive voice or active voice? Maybe you would like to write your book in a less formal tone and make your book more personable, using more practical examples. Take note of the vocabulary in your book and others. Will your audience understand the terms you use? Will you use the same terms as other books? As mentioned, you do not need to read every book out there, only get a good idea. And if you happen to do a considerable amount of reading, be sure to cite your sources if you use any content from others in your book.

Page Count and Trim Size: Word count and page count are frequently overlooked during the writing process. Are comparable titles small or large? Is your book too big or too small for your audience? Does it matter? Many readers prefer a smaller book, while some don't mind a long book. If you are using your book to educate your audience and it's particularly long, you may want to consider writing a series instead of jamming everything into one book. This can also be true for novels and memoirs.

Price: Check the price of similar books on Amazon or other booksellers. The price of your book should be comparable to similar books on the market. Unless your book comes with additional products or services, the price should align with similar titles. Writers can easily price themselves out of the current market, which would make your book less attractive to readers. Just remember, if your price is higher than others, make sure it's for a good reason.

Statistics: You should research how well your genre is doing. Try using Statista or Pew Research studies when checking publishing statistics. Is the type of book you're writing selling well on Amazon or in the United States? This is good to know ahead of time so you'll know whether or not you have a long or short road to turning a profit. You will need to decide if this self-publishing endeavor is an investment or a labor of love. Once you have a good idea of how books in your genre sell, you can track how those books are being marketed, which channels are being used, and which publications they are featured in.

Marketing: How are similar books being marketed? The various ways you can market include direct mail, email marketing, newsletters, pitches to media, book reviews, social media ads/posts, traditional ads, social media influencers, podcasts, radio programming, magazine interviews, word-of-mouth, webinars, blogs, conferences, excerpts from your book published online or in a publication, etc. If you have a strong social media platform that attracts readers and a popular blog or podcast, it will be much easier for your readers to know you are releasing a book. There are also other ways to build an audience that will be different from others. Consider releasing a few small digital products, such as guides, mini courses or master classes.

If you create free and low-cost content, those resources will help you build an email list. Those email subscribers and followers can serve as good ground for your book launch announcement. You could even use your current connections as publicity. Maybe you're a pastor, a physician, a savvy home-schooling mom, president of a ski club, leader in a wellness group or, maybe you sell your own brand of coffee or body balm on Etsy. All those channels give you access to an audience. Keep this in mind. It's easier to market books when you already have a following, so start building interest for your book before it is finished.

STEP 4: TIMING IS EVERYTHING

Publication Date. Most people have heard the term, "timing is everything," but in the book world it could make a huge difference. Aim to publish during a significant date or time. Publishing on a random, insignificant date is like publishing into an unpopulated, dry desert. No one is there watching or paying attention. If you publish during a peak time, readers are more alert and more likely to find content like yours. Strategically set your **publishing date and writing/editing/design schedule** so that your book publishes at the best time. Publishing during holidays or during a peak time for your genre helps to give your book a boost of attention and spotlight. For example, consider February or early summer for relationship books, March/April for textbooks, tax season for business books, and the birthday of a known figure or the anniversary of an important event for historical titles. Other holidays and special dates include:

Prepping for the Bookshelf

Nurses Week	Black History Month
World Mental Health Day	Indigenous People's Day
Mental Health Awareness Month	Fashion Week
Back to School Week	Christmas
Spring Break	Resurrection Sunday/Easter
March Madness	Good Friday
Mother's Day	Ramadan
Father's Day	Hanukkah
Juneteenth	Grandparents Day
Labor Day	Siblings Day
Friday the 13th	Black Friday
Black Music Month	

If your book focuses on an event that gets media coverage, make sure your book is published by that time so that you can pitch it to a news outlet that covers those events, for example anniversaries of major events in history or annual local celebrations. Launching a book during a special event, a holiday or a certain time of year makes a difference because publishing at the right time has always played a key role in getting newly published books as much attention as possible.

To help ensure that you publish at the ideal time, draft a schedule noting each phase of the book development process so you and the people you are hiring can stay on track. Your schedule should include dues dates for attaining writing assistance (if needed) and due dates for reviewers, editors and layout designers. Also include a date for when you will send your work to a printer and find out how quickly they can have print copies ready. Your marketing/advertising, public relations, and pitches to influencers should also go on your schedule.

Average editing timeframes for 40,000- to 50,000-word manuscripts include:

- Ghostwriting: 3–6 months (depending on the complexity of the subject, the amount of research involved, etc.)
- Developmental Editing: 4–8 weeks
- Copyediting: 2–3 weeks
- Proofreading: 1–2 weeks
- Layout design: 2–4 weeks (depending on how much art is included)
- Cover design: 1–2 weeks

STEP 5: DECIDE ON A PUBLISHING FORMAT

Format/Platform. The fifth significant part of your plan is your **publishing method.** There are several options to consider when releasing your book. Do you want to publish in print, audiobook, e-book, interactive e-book or all four? Should you consider Braille? There may be cases in which offering your book in one format to start is a good idea. An e-book only method works well for those on a shoestring budget. It is the cheapest and most convenient way to get your book out there. A reader can download your book to their Kindle, Nook, or iPad and get what they need quickly rather than go through a store to buy a print version. Or they can download a PDF version through your Website or landing page.

Audiobooks have become popular in the last few years. According to Pew Research, one in five readers listen to audiobooks. You can create an audiobook by recording yourself reading your book or hiring voice talent. Uploading options include Audible on Amazon or the Apple Books platform. Despite the popularity of e-books and audiobooks, print books will always be in style. Having a print version available at some point is needed as many readers still love to hold books in their hands and grow their home libraries. Print is still the most popular way to read.

Enhanced or interactive e-books are books that include media such as videos, animations, or motion graphics. They can be especially helpful if you want to appeal to readers who are visual and would enjoy seeing both written and visual content together in one place. A few popular platforms used for creating interactive or enhanced e-books are Apple Books, and Kotobee. Enhanced e-books should be considered if you are writing about something that would benefit from video content or animations, such as some children's books and instructional books. The visuals allow you to provide explicit instructions on how something should be done.

Best Platform Per Book Type

Print

All books should be available in print, but especially these:

Large Art or Coffee Table Books

Print books are needed for all genres, but this is especially true for art and coffee table books. It's hard to appreciate a book with amazing photography when there isn't a print edition. Also, these creative titles often are made using special paper and binding, which can only be featured when printed.

Children's Books

Although a children's book on a tablet can be fun and engaging, many health professionals do not recommend that small children spend a great deal of time reading on screen. It's a good idea to focus on print and then consider enhanced books down the line. Plus, children's books on tablets are best for indoor reading since screens can be difficult to read in the sunlight. Children's books can be read indoors and outside if they are in print.

Cookbooks

A cookbook on a tablet may be convenient for travel, but if you are using it in the kitchen, the tablet can be damaged accidentally due to spills. A hardcopy or paperback is much more resilient.

Workbooks or Books with Fill-in Content

It's frustrating to purchase an e-book that has workbook content. The reader cannot access the fill-in portions. If you have a book that has discussion questions or spaces readers are supposed to complete, create a separate workbook available through your site. The options include creating a fillable PDF for downloading or selling a print copy.

E-books (standard and enhanced)

Novels, Short Stories and Long Textbooks

Works benefiting most from an e-version include reference books and fiction. Fiction writers should consider e-book format because it's portable and allows readers to read while traveling without worrying about size and weight. The same is true for reference books or textbooks. Who wants to lug a 600-page textbook around? And there is software for textbooks that allows students to take notes, bookmark, and mark on a tablet or laptop. Books from the fields of beauty, exercise, science and sports are good candidates for interactive e-books.

Audiobooks

Novels, Memoirs, Inspirational/Spiritual, Self-Help

Any type of book is a good candidate for audiobooks, but memoirs, self-help, and inspirational books can benefit greatly from this format because you can make your story more dramatic. To add excitement, an audiobook is a great option. Hearing the author's words can be more entertaining for readers who may find reading a bit boring. Rather than labor through a long reading list, they may choose audio versions to switch up their usual reading routine and get more books "read." These book lovers can listen while in their cars, relaxing on their front patios, or even sitting in their bathtubs. For some, hearing information rather than reading it can be more memorable and could make a more lasting impression. Audiobooks are also best for those who may struggle seeing or reading. If you want to reach visually impaired readers even more, consider publishing in Braille format.

STEP 6: CREATE A BOOK BUDGET

Budget. An important step in your book-writing plan is your budget. When you estimate costs ahead of time, you will more likely stick to a budget and invest wisely. Publishing a book is like building a house—count the cost, consider everything involved, and add a buffer to account for unexpected emergencies that may arise while developing or launching your book. Begin by gathering estimates for how much each task will cost. Your budget should cover your entire strategy and master plan. Proper budgeting ensures that you don't exceed your profit potential. To start, here are the costs you will need to consider when creating a budget:

Master Planning: Creating a Book-Publishing Plan

- Editorial costs: ghostwriting, writing classes, developmental editing, copyediting, and proofreading
- Reviewers/endorsements (if not free)
- Editorial evaluations or critiques (if solid reviewers are hard to come by)
- Indexing
- ISBNs and barcodes through Bowker or another reputable source (recommended over free ISBNs)
- Design and production costs for cover, interior design, e-book, or interactive e-book platforms
- Printing or manufacturing costs for storing and distributing paperback or hardcover copies (print on demand or a set number of copies)
- Reprint costs and reprint corrections (if you find mistakes after printing)
- Print and online marketing and advertising, social media ads, book trailers
- Videography, photography, and audio-visual editing costs for your Website and any advertising.
- Voice talent for audiobooks (if needed)
- Website for you and your book (can be done yourself if needed)
- Platform for hosting digital supplements such as workbooks, PowerPoint presentations, courses, and other additional resources you may offer along with your book
- Accounting fees for paying taxes on book sales
- Legal fees if you decide to form an LLC or register a DBA with your state. Other costs include a license to operate as a business in your city and possibly business insurance

Plan out your budget and find talent that fits within that set budget. Publishing a book can be a lucrative endeavor or a financial disaster if you do not carefully plan out how much it will cost to publish the book, how much you think you will make selling the book, and how much money you can put in before there's a return on that investment. Your budget can be compared to a publisher's P&L (profit and loss) in that your success lies in how well you plan and anticipate problems. When

17

you self-publish, you are forming a business. Whether or not you need an LLC or a DBA (Doing Business As) depends on your goals. Are you establishing yourself as a publisher? Or is this more of a personal endeavor with plans to publish only one or two books? You can publish in your own name without an LLC and list yourself as the copyright holder on your copyright page. Rules regarding formation vary from state to state so research and remember to note the cost.

You can set up a DBA with business insurance or create an LLC (the type of LLC is typically determined by your accountant). A DBA with insurance or LLC formation will protect and/or separate your business from your assets in case you are ever sued as a result of what you publish. People can and do sue for defamation or copyright infringement—the most common legal issues that pop up in book publishing. This is where having an LLC is helpful. If you are not publishing sensitive content, you may not have to worry about anyone suing you. But create a separate business account for your profits and seek legal counsel and/or an accountant regarding selling books in your state or globally so you know how to manage taxes.

Also, check if your city or township requires business licenses for selling products. A business license may be free, but there may be a fee to register your DBA or LLC with your state. You may also need to set up a tax account in your city. Research your state's Website to get up-to-date numbers on costs and get the latest information on proper protocols and rules. Check the Website of your city as well.

To summarize, budgets keep everything on track, and having one will help you prioritize and plan for success. Determining how much you need to earn and monitoring initial spending will help you make smart decisions about where to put your money. If you don't have a good book to begin with, a good marketing and advertising plan will not help. Budgeting well to develop a high-quality book in the first place will help you market your book with ease.

Step 7: The Path to Book Launch

Marketing and Advertising. Social media has become a staple in the marketing and advertising world. Although it does draw criticism from privacy advocates, social media can be used wisely, and you can pick and choose which platforms you'd like to invest your time and energy. You don't have to be on every social media platform out there, and if you don't already have a social media account, keep it simple by choosing one or two and setting up a business profile. If you'd rather rely on a different type of online presence, you can set up an account on Pinterest, which is primarily a search engine. You can also consider blogging or starting a podcast.

Using online platforms is a great way to build an audience nationally and it's free. If you are currently on social media or Pinterest and you only have personal accounts, upgrade them to business accounts. Setting up business accounts ensures that you see analytics, such as how your posts are doing, how much traffic you're getting, and where your readers are coming from (these upgrades are free). In Goodreads, for example, a top social media site for readers, there is a stats feature, which allows you to track the actions of your readers whether they leave a review or add your book to their list.

You can also consider LinkedIn, Instagram, TikTok (and the hashtag #booktok) Twitter, Facebook, Clubhouse, Patreon and create a YouTube or Twitch. TV channel. There are many different options. Choose one that resonates with you and your audience. From these platforms, you would post relevant everyday-life content, document a few behind-the-scenes moments of your professional life, and share insights from your book. But remember to balance your content. For every book pitch, there should be several posts that share motivational quotes, how-to-content, and encouraging messages or personal stories. This gives readers a chance to get to know you. Also, post a link to your book on all your social media profiles and in your email signature. If you are posting your book on Amazon, the Author Central portal allows authors to post a video, a photo of yourself, and your bio.

Although hiring a marketing team can help, think about success your rate. If you are a newbie, use some restraint on getting all the bells and whistles of an expansive dedicated marketing team. Don't outspend your earning potential. If you are a fairly unknown person, you may want to get assistance for only one or two items and do the rest yourself. You can expand as you go. Once you have a good strategy, you can solicit the help of friends and family to help you execute your plan. There may even be a few interns willing to help you as well.

Advertising, Merchandise Branding and the Author Brand

The range of opportunities to market your book is vast. Video advertising on social media has become a must, but there will be many opportunities to let people know about your book in subtle and bold ways. You can order merchandise that features your book cover and/or a quote from your book. T-shirts, totes, journals, and facemasks are good options. You can pretty much brand anything. You can get your book cover on a bottle of hand sanitizer, a smart phone cover, a jacket, a mug, a water bottle, or a car air freshener. Google branding companies. Many businesses go to these companies to get their company name on all kinds of merchandise for trade shows and giveaways. Choosing items that your readers use often is key.

It's also useful to think about whether or not there is anything mentioned in your book that aligns with a product.

If your book is about an awakening, think about relevant terms like—alertness, revival, and energy. What do you think of when you think of energy? Coffee. Coffee mugs. This is how easily you can brand items that make sense and connect products to your book. Does everything you choose need to have a connection? It doesn't but if something is trending, it may be a good idea to place a quote from your book on it, because if people are using a popular item, they will see your branding every time they use it.

There are many other creative ways you can use to advertise and market. Some will work better than others depending on what you are writing about and your target audience:

- Send postcards
- Create bookmarks
- Give a portion of book sales to your favorite charity
- Write an online brochure or advertorial
- Create book trailers
- Develop a coaching program
- Build courses or master classes
- Digital and social media ads (Facebook, Instagram, LinkedIn, Amazon, YouTube, Twitch.TV, Pinterest, and Google Ads)
- Place billboard ads
- Submit an excerpt to a magazine
- Buy magazine and newspaper ads
- Be a guest blogger on a popular blog
- Appear on a popular podcast or radio show
- Start a blog
- Start your own podcast
- Host a virtual summit, workshop, or conference
- Host a live Q&A on social media
- Bundle your book with another book (either another book you wrote or a colleague's book)

- Create a profile on Goodreads
- Place a sticker on the rear window of your car
- Shrink wrap your car
- Buy an ad on a bus or train
- Buy TV, radio, or podcast advertising
- Pitch to media for a TV segment on a popular news program
- Host book giveaways
- Reach out to book clubs and subscription boxes
- Invite a more prominent author to be a co-author
- Buy advertising at movie theaters
- Post a press release
- Present at a high school career day
- Ask an interior designer if your book can be displayed when they stage homes
- If you know a car dealership manager and your book is car-related, ask if you can donate a book to their waiting rooms
- Donate your book along with other old books to a used bookstore
- Participate in virtual or public readings on social media
- Sponsor an event in your neighborhood
- Buy audio ads through Amazon Advertising
- Advertise through Bookshop.org, Booksy or BookBub
- Create a book club bundle that includes discussion questions, interviews, challenges, activities, games, recipes and other bonuses

Most indie authors know that they need a marketing and advertising plan, but it can take a while to discover which methods work best. There isn't one magic way, and many methods don't work for everyone. Using your research from **Step 3: Learning the Marketplace** and reviewing the many options will help you narrow it down. You can spend a fortune on advertising and marketing and not necessarily sell many books. There are no guarantees in publishing, but successful self-published authors who have earned multiple six figures for more than one book can also be a source of information. But sometimes it truly is about playing the odds to figure out what's working and what isn't.

Book publishers, however, often rely on certain standards to help them earn maximum profits. Until that standard fails, they will typically stick to the tried and true. You can adopt these same methods as a starting point for your own book projects. For example, one method is gaging popularity. Publishers often pay attention to the strength of the author—writing skills, popularity, capabilities, and reputation. All these strengths essentially become a part of the author's personal brand. When a publisher taps into that, it is of great benefit. The advantage to publishing someone with a strong author brand means the publisher is working with an immediately recognizable author, which is why it's easier for celebrities to land a six- or seven-figure book deals with traditional publishers. While your book-writing plan is essential to successful book development and book launch, your branding strategy helps you solidify your position in the book world. It encompasses all that you are as an author.

Your face, your energy, your content and your style are a part of your author brand and anything you do should be an extension of that. We will go into author branding more in Chapter 6, ***The Author Brand: Your Prose Is Your Platform.*** Your author brand is what will often drive your sales. If you can identify it early on, it will help you draft a solid strategy for everything you do before, during, and after your book is written—your planning, writing, marketing, advertising, and platform building are all interconnected. The post-publishing process and proper planning lay the groundwork for profit building. It is the master plan that helps you manage all aspects of your book project with heightened awareness. But in order to effectively execute your plan, you must have a good book to market, and in order to ensure that your book leaves a good impression, you will need to master several aspects of book development.

Chapter 2

Book Anatomy: Building a Book from Concept to Draft

There are several different approaches authors can use when writing a book. For writing nonfiction, some start with writing in a journal or notebook, while more structured authors will focus on drafting an outline. Other approaches include using material you already have, such as a lecture, course or presentation. There isn't one way to get from point A to point B, but there are advantages and disadvantages to each approach.

Drafting Your Book Outline

Using an outline will help you map out a plan for writing your book. A traditional outline is made up of numbered headings and subheads. Outlines provide structure and order for your book. For the structured author, the outline is a reliable blueprint. If you start with an outline, it will be easier to stay organized and keep track of everything you plan to cover. That's easier said than done because many writers prefer to write organically—get everything down on paper and worry about order later.

If your style centers on structure and order, there are several methods you can use to begin writing an outline: 1) you can copy the format of a well-received book and use it as a model, or 2) use idea mapping.

Traditional and Templated Outline Models

The easiest way to create an outline is to follow an example. Find a book similar to the one you want to write; notice how the TOC (Table Of Contents) is written and notice how the chapters are organized. Analyze it, notice where there are gaps in content coverage, and check for unanswered questions. All this information will help you decide on how much you want to cover and how you will make your book completely different. Consider incorporating a similar order in your manuscript using the structure of the other book as a guide.

Idea Mapping

To create an idea map, write down your main subject in the middle of a blank piece of paper or on a white board. Then draw lines connecting the subject to the related topics. Next, you will take each topic and create a list of subtopics. Each subject will represent a chapter you plan to cover. The topics will be covered in subsequent paragraphs. Your subject bubble should include a brief description of the subject you are covering. Using the idea map, you will begin constructing a table of contents. Idea maps are best for writers who find it easier to visualize their book before they begin writing.

Subject Breakdown

If you form chapters using the idea-mapping model, you will have a visual aid that will allow you to see your book as a whole and as a body of many parts. For example, if you are an educator and your subject is "effective communication," you would go through each aspect of what effective communication looks like and cover topics, such as nonverbal communication. What is nonverbal communication? What are good examples of nonverbal communication? What messages get communicated through nonverbal body language? Use the beginning paragraphs to discuss the research and the theories that support your understanding of the subject. Then, you would repeat that system for each form of communication: written, verbal, etc.

In outline building we want to go from big to small; address a complex subject, take it apart, and make it easier for readers to digest. Think about what people know very little about and over explain each facet of that subject. Over explaining ensures that your reader has a greater understanding of it, but the amount of explaining is determined by—remember—your objectives and goals and the age/background of the target audience. What do they need to know given the purpose you have for this book? It's easy to get carried away and this can sometimes lead to redundancy and rambling.

Breaking down your subject lays the foundation for helping readers understand more complex ideas. After you've done this, you can generate a TOC from your completed idea map. Here is an example of chapter organization for a short book on effective communication:

- How to Communicate Effectively in a Crisis
- Introduction
- Chapter 1: Different Forms of Communication
- Verbal communication
- Definition and examples of verbal communication
- Best practices in practicing verbal communication
- Nonverbal communication
- Definition and examples of nonverbal communication
- Best practices in practicing nonverbal communication

- Written Communication
- Definition and examples of written communication
- Best practices in writing effectively

From there, you would customize for your target audience. Does the audience already have a basic knowledge of communication? Are you speaking to adults, children or employees? Is the communication location specific, such as effective communication in a boardroom? Is this a non-profit boardroom or a corporate boardroom? Does it matter?

These types of questions determine how large or small your book will be. The more you focus on your audience, the more you will recognize what readers need to know and what they already know. How can effective communication help? How does this information help readers in a crisis? This is where your objectives and the needs of your audience take center stage, and you begin revising and rewriting the topics covered.

Idea Mapping Through Journaling

Idea mapping can also be done through journal writing. There are two ways you can approach idea mapping through journaling. One way is to grab a blank notebook and use it as a tear sheet scrapbook. Jot down thoughts, summaries, and bits of content. Later, tear them out and begin reordering them and create an outline from there. This approach is a good way to figure out if, in the end, you actually have a book or if you'd much rather turn it into a script, a poetry collection or an article. Not every idea you have will end up being a book idea, but that's the beauty of writing. You may start out going in one direction but end up somewhere else.

The second way to idea map is to journal. Each day you would write out an important point you'd like to cover in your book. Each entry would represent a chapter or a chapter segment, which makes it easier to organize and revise later because your ideas are written together rather than broken down in smaller chunks, such as with other forms of idea mapping. Then take your journal, sort through what you've written, and create a table of contents.

If you find yourself struggling to write new material, start with what you know. It's easier to pick up a good writing pace when you're writing what you know. You're less likely to experience writer's block. Let the ideas flow. Sometimes writers spend too much time overthinking every idea they have. Don't get stuck in your head. You will sort through it all later during the revision process, which we will discuss more in the section on the editorial process.

Idea Mapping Using Transcripts and Presentations

If you are a speaker or teacher, you can take a recorded workshop or presentation and craft a book out of it. One of the best ways to reorganize from a transcript is to idea map all the points you made in your presentation and group the subjects and topics together so you can expound further and form chapters. Presentations can create useful guidebooks or handbooks. One point to keep in mind is that sometimes an organic approach can leave you with so much unordered data that it can be overwhelming and can leave you feeling frustrated. One way to avoid this is to tackle one chapter at a time rather than focusing on the entire book, and the second way is to hire a developmental editor to do this for you.

Revising Ideas: Writing Various Versions

When you sit down to write your first draft, it's important to think about different versions or approaches. Should you rewrite your draft using humor or without? Should one version include personal stories or historical events? Should your book have sidebars? Your memoir may resonate better as a devotional. Consider writing various versions of your draft: funny, serious, simplistic, sarcastic, heavily detailed, one with pictures or without, etc. Think of it like this: In business, visionaries will design various prototypes and versions of a product so that their creativity remains fluid. They create many versions of something to get to a much more effective version with each new design they create. Thinking of or writing out different versions of your book helps prevent you from prematurely releasing a book that's too rough for publication. As noted in the *Business Model Generation* by Alexander Osterwalder and Yves Pigneur, developing models helps you refine your ideas. Even though we're talking about the writing and editing process and not business models, we can apply this truth to the creative process. All art goes through some type of refinement, whether it's pottery, painting, or poetry.

> "If you freeze an idea too quickly, you fall in love with it. If you refine it too quickly, you become attached to it and it becomes very hard to keep exploring [or] keep looking for better. The crudeness of early models in particular [are] deliberate."
>
> –Jim Glymph, Gehry Partners

So, it must be said—the "get rich quick" idea of writing a book in 30 days is a bit of a farce. Yes, you can create a draft in a short timeframe, but usually, the revision process can take anywhere from a few weeks to a few months. Complex projects can take years to finish. In fact, you could, after all of this exploring, find that your nonfiction book works better as a children's book, a collection of flash fiction, or a workbook.

BOOK CASE STUDY

Is there a formula to writing a good book?

If you study great books that have sold millions of copies and continue to sell copies decades after the first printing, you will notice a few basic things. You will notice the average page count for these books, the subject matter, the reading level, the quality of the editing and even the author's ability to solves a reader's problem. Many authors focus on problem solving but not always. If you're trying to solve a problem, you will need to examine it closely. How will you accomplish this? How much of an impact are you really making? Are you solving life/death issues? Are you enabling a reader to move from poverty to wealth? And how long are you taking to explain it all (short book vs. long book)? Are you releasing a course to expound further?

When you think of books you know sold millions of copies, which books come to mind? A few books I'm thinking of didn't publish last year, the year before last or even five years ago. You may have a book like this on your shelf. The book that comes to mind for me is *The Five Love Languages*. This book has become a classic. Let's take a closer look at *The Five Love Languages* by Gary Chapman. It's important to note that many books like this are around 40,000 to 50,000 words and this one was first published in the 90s. *The Five Love Languages* has been on the New York Times Best Seller's list for over 300 weeks and counting. Let's take a look at what you can learn from a book like this.

Prepping for the Bookshelf

First, this isn't a long book. Unless you are writing an incredibly comprehensive textbook, a thrilling novel, or a autobiography/memoir, your book shouldn't be much longer than 50,000 words. In order to determine your manuscript's final page length, you will need to consult with a book layout designer who can assess your manuscript and calculate page count. For example, a 139-page, double-spaced manuscript won't be 139 pages when printed. Using a word count, typesetters can recommend a layout to meet a page count goal (they consider trim size, margin size, font size, spacing between lines, number of images, one-, two- or three-column layout, features, such as side bars, diagrams, or bulleted lists, and the amount of white space or blank pages between chapters). Some memoirs can reach 100,000 or 130,000 words and there are large 400-page books that can sell well depending on the popularity of the author or the subject. But some books are unnecessarily long. Many authors are adamant about pouring everything they have into one book. But the worst thing an author can do is give readers a 100,000-word book, when you can say what you need to say in 60,000 words. You want your book to stick to the main objective, be succinct, be clear and be impactful. Let's look at *The Five Love Languages* a bit more.

What is it about *The Five Love Languages* that keeps this book selling year after year? It's the way he packaged his results. The author provided a solution to a common problem that impacts millions of people. He set out to help fix broken or struggling marriages by incorporating what he came to understand as a marriage counselor. He focused on one very specific point—love. Then, he implemented a system to help couples. He called his method *The Five Love Languages*. Even more, he clearly explained his method; it was concise, to the point, and provided concrete examples and assessments. And he didn't stop there; he released other editions of that book for singles, kids, parents, and the military. One book turned into several. His book could be read in a day or two, and readers could implement what he was telling them right away.

I believe many writers have implemented similar tactics in their own writing, and you can do the same. As you develop content, you want huge impact in a short amount of time, and that requires being in tune with your target audience—know their biggest problem inside out and offer a solution. Not one you necessarily figured out in one weekend. Addressing these kinds of problems may take years; it takes hours of research and hands-on implementation. But that is why this book makes for a great case study, and there are books in other genres that have had a similar effect. People want proven solutions or even something much simpler—they want to get something out of it, such as peace, joy, satisfaction, etc. What is it that you know? How common of a problem is it? How many other people are already solving this problem? Even better: how can you use your knowledge to help people, make them laugh, and give them tools they can apply. Or maybe you'd like to tell them a story that helps them feel better. Even though we are talking about a book that has brought the author a great deal of money, decide early on if profit is your goal. Remember your goals from Chapter 1, you don't have to write for the sole purpose of making money. You can write for the sake of getting your message out or write to share your heart, your life.

The Development of Fiction

When it comes to fiction, development and story structure are much more organic, but the creation of story boards, character sketches, and timelines serve as a way to track the progression and breakdown of all story elements. For some, storytelling comes so naturally that there is no need to create something as definitive as an outline, but fiction authors should keep track of story objectives and how the setting, point of view and plot development all work together to tell a good story. Depending on your goals that could mean a crazy good, inspiring, compelling, imaginative, or easy-to-follow story. Reading amazing works of fiction with various styles and approaches helps fiction authors draft stories that become instant classics.

When deciding on a topic, consider perusing newspaper headlines and history books, and as with nonfiction, check out what is selling. Even though your book project can be a labor of love not bogged down or dictated by budgets, stats, or opinions, other books can be a source of inspiration and serve as a template for building complexity into your story or creating memorable characters.

Characters

When it comes to characters, multidimensional or complex characters keep readers interested. Characters cause readers to think, act, and reflect. Evoking emotion and allowing characters to make predictable and unusual choices causes readers to wonder what comes next. Readers are anxious to find out what will become of their beloved characters—characters that they have grown to like, love, or understand. Creating characters that readers care about is a major goal in writing a good story.

Plot

In organizing your plot, pay attention to the pacing of your story and how quickly a problem resolves or escalates. A fast-moving story may leave out too many details and confuse readers while a slow-moving story can leave readers bored and disinterested.

Point of View/Narration

Whether you use an omniscient narrator, first person narrator, or maybe your narrator is a child, your point of view impacts how the story unfolds. If your story is told in the first person, your narrator doesn't know everything, so the viewpoint of the narrator should be one of discovery. In contrast, the omniscient narrator knows all. If you plan to bring on an editor while you are writing, he or she can help keep you on track with this. How your story is told should make sense.

General Storytelling

If you are writing a memoir or a biography and you are covering a wide range of events, be sure to organize your thoughts first. Think about your objectives: why are you writing a memoir? Why are you writing about a person? What events should you share? What will resonate with readers and why? Many authors begin without thinking about the objective, the end goal. The reader is an afterthought and what is in the author's heart is at the forefront. When there's a view point that includes the heart of the author and the heart of the reader, authors have a better chance at creating page-turning books or books that inspire readers. Imbalance creates disconnect and frustration. Keep both the reader and the author's point of view in mind. Remember, your story could compel someone to keep going. Your fiction could inspire deep, meaningful dialogue among friends or strengthen relationships.

When it comes to creative nonfiction, such as memoir, autobiography, or biography, there needs to be a concerted effort to maintain order. Like we established above with fiction writing, there are various elements you must pay attention to because writing about real people or writing about ourselves can involve long-term research. The problem that often arises when writing these types of books is that you may end up creating never-ending projects. You work on a book for several years and end up with a mess of research that isn't in a form that readers can easily digest or appreciate.

To avoid this issue, you can implement a two-step approach to manage the writing process—a termed plan for writing and a termed plan for research. Storing your work in your closet or on your hard drive doesn't lead to a written book. So start by creating a research plan where you will take time to write out various events or occurrences that were pivotal moments. You may need to interview a few people or visit a library or research site. Create folders for your research and separate them by topic or purpose. You are not writing a book at this point. This process of researching and gathering information could last months or years, so take notes but do not start any chapters. Not writing chapters at this point will help you organize later.

The next step is to create a one-year writing plan with a start date and an end date. The reason for separating writing from research is that when you combine the two, you can easily lose track of what you're doing. You don't want to write something full of gaps, holes, redundancy, or there are too many events out of order. Not everything you discover while researching will end up in your book. So try writing after research. You may find that you are more prepared to write after you have completed your research—when the flow of ideas is too strong to put on the back burner. This is when reviewing your research can be more useful—you now have everything you need to begin writing chapters and creating a table of contents.

Consider separating writing from pure research as much as possible. When someone spends many years writing and researching at the same time, they may end up with a mishmash of information that has not been sorted through properly. When that happens, many things get lost. Your message or theme for the book gets lost. You may end up focusing on the wrong things and have too many missing pieces. You can't see the forest through the trees because both the writing and the research process have bogged you down. You can't see that it's becoming its own thing—an unmanaged blob of data and not a book. An expert writer can sometimes successfully work their way through this, but for a novice writer, it becomes too overwhelming to manage. This is where the review process becomes essential, whether you use editors, fellow authors, or engage in a peer-review process. Because at the end of it all, whether you are writing fiction or nonfiction, there comes a point in your process where another pair of eyes is helpful. There are a few ways you can go about getting reader feedback.

How to Obtain Audience Feedback: The Art of Peer Review

During your writing process, you may go through several drafts before you begin thinking about the next phase of the process, which is gathering feedback. After you've completed your first official draft, you are ready to have another pair of eyes review your manuscript. You could skip this process and go straight to editing, but I encourage new and experienced authors to choose at least two or three people to review your manuscript. In selecting someone to review your work, keep in mind that there are three types of reviewers: beta readers, peer reviewers, and endorsers. A peer review will come from professional colleagues working in the same field as you or fellow writers creating in the same genre. These peer reviewers are sharing their professional opinion or expertise. They provide detailed feedback on what's missing or outdated. They are educated or experienced professionals who may also be authors themselves.

A beta reader reads the book from the perspective of your ideal audience. Your beta reader will tell you if your writing is too boring or not interesting enough or lacks originality. A beta reader, more or less, is sharing his or her personal opinion. Your ideal beta reader should already be a reader of books and not a random person. If they are not already reading books on a regular basis, they may not be able to give you the feedback you need. Beta readers are avid readers that can articulate why they like certain books more than others. You want a reader who can give you details. This is someone who, after reading a book, can tell you detail by detail why she or he liked a book and why it resonated well. A reviewer or beta reader should never tell you, "This is great," without giving you details about why your book is great. No book is perfect, so your feedback should vary from "This book is amazing because it's easy to read," to "I didn't understand the last paragraph in Chapter 2." Beta readers can be your friends, but you should have at least one or two who can serve as objective readers.

As for endorsers, there are two types. The first type is a prominent individual who can provide professional feedback and offer an endorsement you can use for your back cover, Website, or marketing collateral. Let's call them tier-one endorsers. Endorsers are brought in at the end of the book development process. You would contact an endorser once you have a "near final" draft and completed at least one round of copyediting. The benefit to getting endorsers is that their reputation can help influence and grab the attention of readers. For an endorsement you can approach prominent authors, professors, *New York Times* bestselling authors, industry leaders, well-known speakers, and editors-in-chief of newspapers or magazines to review and comment on your book. A tier-one endorser has an opinion that holds weight. Those reviews can serve as great confidence boosters and you can use their positive reviews in your marketing campaigns. In addition, if you get any unfavorable reviews pointing out one or several missteps, you can use that information as a part of your revision strategy. Any opportunity to fix your book before it is published is a great opportunity.

The second type of endorser comes from a prominent organization, such as *Publisher's Weekly*. Professional reviews from organizations can be included on your front or back cover. If you're able to acquire a long list of positive reviews, you can create a "Praise" section in your front matter listing all the quotes from reviewers.

Some authors may wonder, "Do I need to solicit reviews from peer reviewers, beta readers, or endorsers?" Although every author can benefit from peer reviewers, beta readers and endorsers, each person can approach the review process in various ways. For example, a textbook can benefit from peer reviewers (other professors or educators), beta readers (such as students in your field of study), and endorsers (prominent institutions or organizations). With a memoir you may lean toward beta readers and if you are writing biography or historical fiction you may lean heavier on peer reviewers who are history buffs or history teachers. Endorsers are helpful for any type of book because positive reviews can boost your marketing.

Below is a list of professional organizations you can contact for reviews. Some will review for free while others charge a fee. Not all of these organizations will guarantee a review once they've received a copy of your book. If they accept, expect a review time period of 4 to 10 weeks or longer. Some offer expedited reviews at a higher cost:

NetGalley
Kirkus Indie
African American Review (solicited only)
Publisher's Weekly
Foreword/Clarion
Library Journal
Booklist
Self-Publishing Review

School Library Journal
Indies Today
BlueInk
OnlineBookClub.org
Book Reporter
IndieReader
New York Times Book Review
Rain Taxi

COLLECTING FEEDBACK FROM BETA REVIEWERS AND PEER REVIEWERS

In gathering feedback for your manuscript, you should write out a list of questions to ask your reviewers. It's best to use a questionnaire generator such as SurveyMonkey, Google Forms, or Typeform to create your survey. Then, you can email the questions to your reviewers. You should send your questions along with instructions and include a chapter, a few chapters, or the entire book. Ideally you want at least three reviewers for the entire book. If you find a particular chapter is problematic select two or three reviewers to look at that specific chapter. Keep in mind; you can customize your approach to this. You may ask some reviewers to read the entire book, while selecting one or a few people to read certain chapters. For an example list of questions, you can ask reviewers, see Appendix A at the back of this book.

Essentially, you can use any combination of reviewers: one peer reviewer and two beta readers, or one peer reviewer, one beta reader, and one endorser/professional reviewer. There's no limit to how many beta readers, peer reviewers, and endorsers you can have, but sometimes casting your net too wide can make the process more complicated with you wading through endless reviews. Doing this will make it harder for you to finish your book. Reviewers are guides; don't let the process completely derail or delay your writing process. For tier-one endorsers you should leave space on the questionnaire for them to share additional thoughts and include their endorsement.

In your instructions you should give your reviewers a deadline for when you need their feedback. It is good practice to include an incentive to not only encourage them to read your work in a timely manner but to also thank them for their time. In the corporate book-publishing world, publishers often offer various amounts for peer reviews. Self publishers can expect to pay the same or less. Beta readers are the least expensive option Also, send thank-you cards and free copies of your book when it's released. If you are asking for a critique or a manuscript evaluation from an editor, the cost is a bit higher and varies depending on the length and complexity of your book.

There are few methods you can use to find beta readers, peer reviewers, and tier-one endorsers:

Seven Ways to Find Beta Readers

- Find readers at local writers' groups or book clubs (meetup.com, libraries, cafes, book stores, etc.)

- Hold your own readers' circle at your local church, a small café, inside your home, or online

- Make connections at local networking events

- Attend conferences or retreats virtually or in person (e.g., 20 Books Vegas, IBPA events, etc.) to meet people who would be interested in reading your content. Acquisitions editors and literary agents can also be found at conferences

- Ask an editor to serve as a beta reader or peer reviewer

- Contact book reviewers that work for newspapers, magazines, journals or run their own book blog. You can also find bookstagrammers on Pinterest and Instagram that review books. They may even help you with sales and promotion by featuring your book on their platform

- Reach out to book-loving personalities who have their own podcast or YouTube channel

This feedback will help you identify any glaring omissions, major organizational issues, and bring any content inaccuracies to your attention. Your goal is to determine if more content is needed or if anything needs to be rewritten. You may even discover that your book should go in a different direction. Having your book workshopped with beta readers, peer-reviewers, or tier-one endorsers can help you further refine your content and validate your book idea. If you obtain good feedback, you can decide what your next step will be—revise your book further or move on to the next phase of the editorial process.

Some may feel that allowing feedback or reading the work of other authors will sway them too much or taint what they are doing. It's a valid concern, and you may find it best to be a lone wolf in the book-writing process permanently or for a time. But consider this: reviewing, researching and gathering feedback will push you to create something better. As I pointed out in Chapter 1 under reviewing competition or similar authors, hiring reviewers isn't about validation, it's about positioning yourself for attention. And the uniqueness or originality of what you create is a part of branding, which I will continue to discuss throughout this book.

If you're a new author and you're still rather uncomfortable sharing your work for whatever reason (maybe there's a pending patent or trademark; maybe there's sensitive content; or maybe you are worried about the nefarious intentions of others), you might consider asking your beta reader or peer reviewer to sign a non-disclosure agreement. This may turn readers off, but most professional peer reviewers have signed them many times before. If you still find it difficult to find trustworthy eviewers, here are two recommendations:

1. Ask an editor to serve as a reviewer. Preferably you want an editor who specializes in both your genre and subject matter. He or she can critique your book with your audience in mind. Since editors are already used to working with contracts, they are more willing to sign non-disclosures, and most editors include confidentiality clauses in their own agreements anyway.

2. Use reviews from organizations only. It's unusual for an organization like *Publisher's Weekly* to undercut your success.

Carefully selecting who sees your work protects your manuscript from being shared too broadly without adequate protection. For more information on copyrights and protecting your work see Chapter 5.

Chapter 3

Book Editors 101: What They Do and How They Do It

Now, we've come to a stage some may call the coup de grâce—working with editors. You may be entering this stage of the process with excitement or dread. Many writers have had bad experiences working with editors and may feel apprehensive about working with one again. But building a stable, lasting relationship with an editor will help you stress less about the publishing process. They will be your champion and your extra pair of eyes. There are so many aspects of publishing that book editors can expose you to. You'll become a pro at deciding on everything from paper quality to printers, to trim size and book covers. Writing and publishing books will become second nature once you become more familiar with the editorial and production process, which includes working with ghostwriters, developmental editors, copy editors, line editors, proofreaders, permissions editors, editors serving as project managers, and layout/cover designers.

There are two points at which you can invite an editor into your process. You can include them at the very beginning, allowing them to help you flesh out your book ideas and discover your target audience. Or you can bring an editor in after you've been through peer reviews and beta reads. Using an editor early on means that you will get from point A to point B faster because a professional will be assisting you. They have insight and a wealth of information at their disposal. It creates a more seamless process. It may not be possible to work with someone early on, because finding a good editor that you click with may not come so easily. But you definitely want to plug an editor in before sending your manuscript out to tier-one endorsers (people you want to sing your praises). But keep in mind: the more work you need, the more expensive the editing becomes. This is why peer reviews and beta reads will help you tremendously. Readers don't necessarily review your work with an editor's eye, but they can uncover issues you didn't notice.

Meeting an editor often begins through one of several touch points. You may have found someone on social media, at a conference, while shopping in a bookstore, in a Facebook group, or during a random online or in-person event. Editors can be found at professional organizations and sites, such as ACES, the Editorial Freelancers Association, Editors of Color, and more. Although there are numerous editors out there, not all of them will be a good fit for you. You can also find average editing costs through the Editorial Freelancers Association. You'll want to ask about the editor's past experiences. Which book publishing houses did they work for? Where did they get their training? Do they specialize in your genre? How do they work? What do their contracts look like? For more sample questions you can ask editors check Appendix A: Questions to Ask Creative Professionals.

The official editor-author relationship usually begins with an agreement, which outlines the terms of your professional relationship. Editor agreements state when work will begin and what will be performed. An editor agreement should always have a statement that says you are the owner of the work and will remain the owner of the work. A statement about confidentiality should also be included. An editor shouldn't share the details of your story without your consent. It is also worth asking about the editor's home office and level of security if your manuscript includes sensitive or high-profile information. For example, do they use a VPN system or an encrypted portal for uploading sensitive documents? Ask about storage. What happens to copies of your final drafts after the project has ended? Are they stored on a separate hard drive or deleted? How long will the editor store your final drafts and ask if there are any fees involved?

As a writer, you want the best possible experience working with an editor. So before working with one, set realistic expectations. If you don't do this, both you and the editor will end up at odds, and in the end, the book will suffer as a result. During your first meeting with an editor, discuss the editor's approach to editing. Does she take a light, medium, or a heavy hand? What type of books does he or she edit on a regular basis? Is she married to the King's English or is the editor more flexible with certain grammatical rules? You want to establish common ground. Does what you're looking for line up with what the editor is willing to do. Communication and agreement are essential to establishing a healthy author-editor relationship. You have to trust each other and possibly learn to accept an editorial decision you may not like if it's the best thing for the book. This includes adjusting your writing style to fit your target audience.

Expectations are also related to intention. Think about what goes on in an editor's head? Editors are artists too just like writers; they are just on the other side of that narrow line. Editing is an art, not an exact science. When editing, whether it's in a corporate setting or in the freelance world, several questions loom in the mind of editors, especially developmental editors, as they read content: What do you have in common with your audience? Are they educated? Will they understand graduate level writing or basic vocabulary? Is your content region-specific? What are your goals as an author? Editors have goals also. Editing goals can be two-fold. First, eliminate as much error as possible, and second, increase understanding between author and reader. Editors examine issues regarding organization of thought, accuracy and clarity of content, inconsistencies or contradictions in thought, sensitivity, and issues with flow and readability.

The goal is to also find out the following: What's missing? What makes sense? Are all concepts explained? Is the tone appropriate for the audience? Often these questions don't always cross the writer's mind and that is what editors bring to the table. Share with editors what is going on in your head. Allow the editor to know what you are thinking and what direction you'd like to go in. There will be give and take on both sides to get to the goal, which should center on being authentic with the reader—not on the sole perspective of the editor or the writer. After chapters are developed and a first draft is created, editors take you into the throes of the editorial process—revising, rewriting, reorganizing, and re-editing.

THE EDITORIAL PROCESS

What is the Editorial Process?

As stated earlier, the sooner an editor is involved the better off an author is. Writing an entire book only to realize later that an entire rewrite is needed can be discouraging. This can happen to new authors or those who have published before, but that is why there is an editorial process in book publishing—a process to ensure that the book content is clear, fully developed, and with fewer errors. The first step in the editorial process involves the editor performing a manuscript review or an assessment to determine what kind of shape your book is in. This is often called an editorial evaluation or review. (Note: some editors charge a reading fee to assess or review your manuscript) This review will determine what the book needs (more editing, writing, research, etc.) and how much it will cost to edit. There are a few ways an editor can do this. Here is a common approach, which encompasses many areas:

Manuscript Review Can Include:

1. Overall Review

- Content organization: Do chapters need to be reordered? Are topics out of order? Is there a confusing timeline?
- Content coverage: Is further explanation of concepts necessary? Is content coverage balanced for each chapter? Are key concepts missing?
- **Content Accuracy**: How reliable is the content? Does the book have a lot of inconsistencies, old references, and inaccurate assumptions about different cultures? Taking an even deeper dive editors will ask:
  - Are more references needed?
  - Are the sources listed reputable?
  - Are in-text citations or footnotes present?
  - Are there holes in the original research?

2. Review of Style, Reading Level, and Flow

- Measure how easily content is understood by assessing reading level
- Evaluate content flow and style: Are there missing transitions? Are sentences too long?
- Is the style of writing distracting, too flowery, or not substantive enough—not clear, concise and to the point? Do chapters follow a logical flow?

3. Level and Type of Edit

- Does the book require a light, medium or heavy edit?
- Does the book require a developmental edit or can it go straight to copyediting?
- Editors may check the number of misspellings and word choice errors

4. Style Recommendation

❖ Most editors have a preferred style. Formally trained book editors are initially trained in *The Chicago Manual of Style*, which often begins in college through an English degree program, but certification or certificate programs can also teach book editing. Several colleges have established programs in book publishing, and at these schools, English majors can graduate with a concentration in book editing, and also obtain editing experience by completing an internship with a publishing house.

❖ *Chicago* is the standard style in books, but once an editor has begun their career, they learn other styles and may gravitate toward one or a few.

The top style guides editors follow are:

- ❖ *The Chicago Manual of Style (CMOS)*: book editors
- ❖ *Publication Manual of the American Psychological Association (APA)*: nursing, social sciences, some medical professions and psychology editors
- ❖ *Associated Press Stylebook (AP)*: journalists and journalism editors writing for newspapers, magazines, and blogs
- ❖ *American Medical Association Manual of Style (AMA)*: medical practice, medical education editors

As you collaborate, you and your editor will determine which style works best for your project. You can also send your editor a style sheet of key terms, spellings, and writing tendencies you would like preserved during editing. This helps you and the editor stay on the same page as the manuscript goes back and forth from you to the editor and then back to you for revision. Take this opportunity to gather as much information about the editor's style and experience as possible so that you can become comfortable and build a lasting rapport.

5. Confirm Target Audience

- If you are able to choose an editor who has extensive experience in your field, he or she can provide some insight as to whether or not you will effectively reach your target audience.
- Is the content appropriate for the target audience?
- Does the author drift away from the target audience and begin to cover another subject best suited for an entirely different audience?
- Your editor may request an audience profile from the author if the editor has limited experience in the field.

Once an editor has completed his or her review, the editor will set up a time to discuss next steps or send a proposal. During this time, the editor will let you know if you need more development or if copyediting is the next step. If development is needed, the editor will reveal how intense the edit could be. It could be extensive or it could merely focus on filling in a few gaps here and there. Below is a step by step break down of the editorial process.

EDITING STEPS WITHIN THE EDITORIAL PROCESS

Manuscript review
Developmental edit
Author revision
Finalized edit
Copyedit
Author revision
Second round copyedit (if necessary)
Proofread
Interior design layout
Second round proofread
Author review
Designer completes proofreading corrections
Final checks

Not all writers need a developmental editor. Simpler, well-written books may only need copyediting, which includes correcting grammatical errors, poor word choice and editing for improved readability, sensitivity, and clarity. If you don't know whether or not your book needs development, review the following points below. Topics covered here will help you examine your own content.

Effectiveness of Writing Style

One key aspect of effective writing is accessibility—making sure your writing isn't too hard to understand. Always keep your audience in mind when you are describing events or explaining concepts. Years ago one of my English professors said this: "There are people who have PhDs and there are people who want you to know they have PhDs." It's an important point because to be received well by your reader, you want to be understood and you want your reader to "get it." You don't want them to be impressed only by the fancy words you use. You want them to be changed, inspired, better informed, etc. That is how good books are written. The goal should be to relay topics using a writing style that makes it easy for readers to understand what you are saying and follow along with ease.

You also want to be aware of your audience's reading level and education level. Do they read at an eighth-grade reading level? Does your reader have a degree? Also keep in mind that if you use terminology only used by people of a certain locale, you may only reach a limited group of readers. Another good rule of thumb is to avoid using words that are rarely used in everyday conversation. You can be sophisticated without being complicated. Copy editors do fix issues such as poor grammar and long, confusing sentences, but the more you develop the best writing style for your audience on your own, the better off you will be and the fewer rounds of editing you will need.

Organization of Concepts and Topics

Content organization involves many elements—order of events, order of topics, and use of transitions, which is the glue that ties everything together. Order is crucial especially in textbooks and teaching guides. Fiction, autobiographies and memoirs can use flashbacks and focus on beginning with an important memory rather than starting from a person's birth. In nonfiction educational resources, you'll want to pay attention to order when relaying research, defining a concept, explaining an opinion, or providing commentary on a thought, historical event, or current news. Introduce your topic by defining key terms and concepts. Then you can discuss details. Logically progress from topic to topic without abruptly changing the subject. If your chapter focuses on effective business communication, resist the urge to segue into a different topic altogether, such as communication among families. That would be a different book entirely.

Each chapter should cover various aspects of a particular topic, including definitions and examples. If your topic is hard to explain, try using a story or an illustration to help your readers understand. As you progress from one topic to another, use transitions. Transitional phrases will give each chapter a smooth flow. Disjointed content confuses readers.

Depth of Coverage

It's important to consider how deep you want to go when explaining a concept or topic. For example, if you're writing a book on business communication, you should think about which aspect of the topic you'd like to cover. Are you teaching your reader how to communicate in a boardroom or how to give a speech to donors or how non-verbal communication impacts your relationships with co-workers? Depending on the objectives you have set for your book, you may want to focus on one imperative aspect rather than several.

Communication is a very broad topic. You can write several volumes or focus on a key point. In order to decide how much detail you should include, try thinking about your reader's personality type. Is your reader about practicality and getting to the point quickly? Practical readers enjoy shorter books. This is true for most self-help or how-to books. If everything can be said in 150 pages, they'd rather read and recommend that book rather than languish through a 300-page book. People who don't read your book all the way through can't honestly recommend it to others. Book purchases get you sales, but recommendations get you book sales year after year. You want your book to sell well after you've released it.

Also, it's worth mentioning that in nonfiction the subject matter can be researched, verified, and expanded upon by the editor (often independent of the writer), but in fiction and memoir, the story lies within the author. Anything that's confusing or lacking depth needs to be pulled out of the writer. The editor won't know these details.

Clarity in Relaying Key Messages or Thoughts

Your key message or theme is the most important part of your book. When you ramble or cram too much information into your book, you risk losing your reader. When readers get frustrated, they'll put your book down and opt for something simpler. You want to be concise and get to the point without causing confusion. Don't be repetitive. Be clear in your descriptions or explanations and move on to the next topic. Your mission in relaying your key message is to communicate it clearly. Organize your thoughts, use accessible language (common terms, words), and then remind the reader at the end of what you told them. Don't repeat the same thing over and over—define, discuss, provide an example or illustration, and summarize at the end.

Content Accuracy and Currency

There is nothing that frustrates a reader more than inaccurate information. Spend some time researching, fact-checking, or hiring a researcher (degreed developmental editors and copy editors will have a firm grasp on how to research and evaluate sources). Your content should be accurate and current. The resources you reference should be less than two years old, unless you are discussing a theory that has seen little advancement. If your work is original, make sure to note where your perspective falls among similar authors in the field. Make sure you cite your sources and seek permission if you wish to reprint any diagrams or tables that another author created. Writing with integrity and ethics is key to establishing yourself as a reputable authority.

These strategies will help you write a book that has fewer holes and issues. After your book is well developed, you are ready for copyediting. Keep in mind that like many authors you may want to add line editing, which is an edit that focuses on the tone, feel, or effectiveness of the writing and less on the grammar. Many copy editors include this type of review when they are fixing grammar, so you don't need to separate line editing from copyediting. But if you want a review that doesn't focus too heavily on grammar, choose a line editor, then move on to copyediting. Another option is to choose a copy editor who performs line editing. But once you've chosen your editors and you've decided on the type of editing, the revision stage begins. As we covered earlier in this chapter, there are various steps/stages to editing. As you get deeper into the process, you will need to understand how complex this process can be.

REWORKING THE FIRST DRAFT: REVISING AND COPYEDITING

After entering the development and/or copyediting phase, expect a certain amount of back and forth. Both developmental editors and copy editors insert queries or comments when they don't understand something or they want to draw your attention to a heavy change. Adding comments to heavy changes highlights text the author can check to see if the intended meaning was lost. During the revision process, you will work closely with your editor to ensure all queries were addressed and that all edits are acceptable. As you begin the revision process, you'll want to address anything concerning such as over editing or too many errors being introduced. Some authors have had challenging experiences working with editors, but there are three main reasons why I believe editor-author relations deteriorate.

1. Communication breakdown

- Miscommunication between authors and editors occurs because the editorial process doesn't line up with author expectations.

- Not fully covering key details: level of edit (light, medium, heavy), type of edit (developmental, copyediting, proofreading), number of editing rounds, unsupervised outsourced editing (different editors being brought into the process unbeknownst to the author. This includes the process not being reviewed or managed well by the primary editor), time frame for when editing is completed (the editor finished later than expected due to the manuscript needing more work) the process for reviewing editor changes was unclear or not finalized (tracked changes in Microsoft Word was used when the author expected a highlighted PDF)

- Unresponsiveness due to a mishandled crisis, whether personal or business related. This includes using resources to keep you and the editor connected throughout the entire process, an app, calendar, alert system, or the use of an assistant.

- Not informing the editor or author that you have an ongoing illness or if you are caring for a sick loved one.

2. Not using a style sheet

- Editors follow style guides and house style guides specific to a particular organization, but it is helpful for an editor to create a style sheet after reviewing or copyediting a manuscript. Style sheets are created so that the author and editor can note unique spellings specific to the text, colloquialisms, formatting notes, or anything that the author would want the editor to pay extra attention to or avoid changing. These are also used when handing the manuscript off to a proofreader. Also, an editor or an author can contribute to a style sheet.

- Not using a style sheet can result in many unapproved changes being applied to the manuscript. It's a waste of time for the editor to edit only to have most or all changes rejected, and it's an unnecessary source of frustration for the author.

- Style sheets create better synergy between the author and the editorial team as the style sheet gets distributed to each editor when the next stage of the editorial process begins (i.e., developmental editor to copy editor to proofreader to designer). They can also be updated after each phase of editing. The author can better track changes especially if the content is challenging—as is sometimes the case with complex content that includes a lot of features, tables, charts, art, math formulas, or side bars.

3. Poor scheduling

❋ The editing and writing schedule is one of the most important pieces of the editorial process. If materials aren't delivered, there is no book to publish. If the book needs to be present at a conference (virtual or in-person) or published on a specific date, sticking to a schedule is key to the book's success. If an author or editor misses a deadline, it throws everything off.

❋ One way to stay on track is to sync your schedule with a shared calendar where everyone can see the dates. Setting up reminder alerts will keep everyone organized and on track.

❋ If you've asked your editor for help with permissions, request permission forms early. Since permissions can take several weeks to go through, start sending those out as soon as possible. Also request a photo release form for any photos in your book that feature close-ups of people. It's a good practice to provide permissions instructions or licensing information on your author Website for any one/organization that wants to adapt your book's content for a program or special project.

4. Lack of project management

❋ Ideally there should be more than one editor reviewing your book. Development editors are typically head editors since projects often begin with them. Authors should budget for two to three editors per manuscript (three is better). One to handle development, one to handle copyediting, and one to handle proofreading, with the developmental editor coordinating, checking progress and reviewing work during each stage. Many self-published authors often expect one editor to catch all the errors and manage all phases of development, but that is an unrealistic expectation. One editor will not catch all errors. To put this in perspective, at a publishing house, four to seven editors on average have edited the same manuscript, not including reviewers and beta readers. Some of those editors may have even read the manuscript more than once.

❈ Also, it's worth noting that in the corporate book publishing space, this process is typically managed by a project editor/manager who would ensure a smooth workflow from editor to editor and to design, marketing, and manufacturing. For self-published authors, many developmental editors also act as project managers. They will often bring in their own teams to help edit and design your book. If they prefer, authors can take the lead on this process too. Using a qualified project manager cuts down on miscommunication and confusion.

In closing, editors can contribute and share ideas in addition to editing. They ask questions, consult, manage, and dig deep into your head. They may even encourage the exploration of themes and symbolism as you work through your manuscript. But as a self-published author, you are in control over how everything is planned and executed. Creatives can be involved with everything—the nuts and bolts and small details. Or, they can serve only as an "alongsider," giving you general advice with little day-to-day involvement. With experience you will know how to best use creatives, but if you are a newbie remember your master plan, set goals, and ask questions. Take your time getting to know people and the publishing process so you can develop a strategy that works well with your goals and objectives in mind.

Chapter 4

Art, Covers, and Layout Design: Working with Designers

When your manuscript has been fully developed and edited, you can begin the layout design process, also known as book formatting. You will discuss final page count, font size and style, spacing between the lines of text, and the size of the margins with a layout designer. As a self-published author, you'll have complete control over how the layout looks. Is the font size too small for your audience? Are the margins too slim? Layout design for print and e-book can be done yourself if you are willing to learn and master the process. There are a number of tools you can employ, such as InDesign, Vellum, Apple's Pages and BookWright. But if you are including art, tables, diagrams or boxed features and lists, it's best to hire a professional to avoid complications like art resizing issues, reflow problems, and glitchy software. Even if you are motivated to design your own book, using a professional will ensure a more polished look. Design professionals know the ins and outs. It will take them less time and effort to create a flawless design. Be sure you've covered all your bases before layout design by following a few key points:

1. Stock art is cheaper short term but not long term. When you're self-publishing, it is much more cost-effective to get original art work created, whether that involves taking photos yourself or hiring an illustrator to create art for you. These images can be used over and over without restrictions. In addition, if you use your own photos or art, you can license your art or charge permission fees to gain a little extra revenue.
2. For print, art needs to be submitted to your printer at a high resolution of at least 300 DPI (dots per inch) so make sure you and your designer are working with high-resolution files. This is especially important for book covers. Art that is suitable for printing are uncondensed, raw art files
3. Keep track of art by completing an art log that contains the name and number of the image that corresponds to the call out (or place holder) in the manuscript. This tells the designer where the art goes. Art logs should also include the legend or caption and any notes regarding any permission fees or issues, before sending it to the designer.

Book Covers

Each part of the book cover is significant. The front, back, and spine should stand out with punches of color and bold graphics and type. The front cover is your calling card and a great way to show off a dazzling design that features a clear, catchy title, and a reviewer comment. Although the front cover is often the most important part of the cover online, the spine is usually the first part of the cover readers see in a bookstore or library. Your front cover won't always be seen right away, so you should ensure that the spine is just as attractive as the front cover. The spine is an extension of the front cover design. What is exciting, fresh, and appealing about your front cover should extend into the spine.

Your back cover, which should include a brief summary of your book (a blurb), a few comments from professional reviewers, a photo of you and your author bio should be proofread. The copy should be easy to read, so avoid small fonts and black backgrounds. If you release a hardback version of your book with a book jacket, you will have more room to include more copy on the inner flaps. Let's dive deeper into different approaches to book cover design.

Four Types of Book Covers

There are four main types of book covers: abstract, photographical, illustrative, and typographical. Designers use abstract elements, photos, custom illustrations, and various font sizes and types to create dynamic stand out covers. Although cover design is subjective, pay attention to the cover designs of popular books and listen to reader feedback and reviews. What you think is an amazing cover may not necessarily resonate well with your readers. Consider choosing a professional book cover designer who can deliver a design comparable to industry standard, well-liked covers. Doing so will help your book stand out and it will look just as good as books published through a commercial book publisher like Simon Schuster or Random House.

Abstract

Computer-generated graphics created through Photoshop or some other graphics program are used to create abstract covers that feature geometric shapes and swirling colors. Abstract covers give books an industrial, surreal or transcendent feel. Textbooks, academic titles and quirky books can use abstract designs as a backdrop for a design that includes mathematical symbols, art deco styles, or post-modern design elements. Abstract images can also blend with human form to coincide with the content of the book. For example, a sci-fi book may choose an abstract cover that shows a galaxy with a detached head floating through the stars. Abstract designs are often computer generated but you can also use abstract art for your cover.

Photographical

One or several photos can serve as the main artistic element on photography-based covers. Photos can be black and white or in color. You could include a photo of yourself, other people, your family, a mural, or a colorful landscape. Photos can even be layered like a collage, blurred or set into the background and spread across the entire cover.

Illustrative

An original drawing can help you separate your book from others. These covers incorporate hand-drawn landscapes, figures, and other objects. Illustrations can be used for a wide variety of titles including children's books, poetry, and fiction. Illustrative covers feature original works and can lend itself to a more original cover design. Illustrations can be black and white sketches, digitized water color or acrylic paintings, and even chalk drawings.

Typographical

These cover designs display the book title in large font to fill up much of the space. It's a style used in memoirs, self-help titles, inspirational books, and those that want to emphasize words and letters. Words can be repeated or written multiple times across the page. The large title may even feature other elements such as floral patterns or bright colors. Typographical books use words as the primary design element. They can be enhanced by other elements like photos or illustrations, but not overshadowed by those images. Large font designs work well with short titles.

All four of these design approaches can be used separately or together to create bold and attractive covers, but what adds even more personality and punch to a book's cover design is color.

Use of Color in Cover Design

There are four main types of color choices for covers: one color, two color, four color, and sepia. Four color is preferred because you can incorporate all the colors of the rainbow. Most, if not all, commercial publishers use a four-color cover. Because printing in four-color is more expensive, textbook, academic, or small publishers on a shoestring budget may use a one-color interior design with a four-color cover.

Authors who are self-publishing should invest in a four-color cover because you can create whatever design you want without limitations. Although there are major distributors that will not carry your book if it doesn't have a four-color cover, other less colorful designs have done well in the marketplace due to the strength and reputation of the author. Covers such as Jamaica Kincaid's *The Autobiography of My Mother* and *Between the World and Me* by Ta-Nehisi Coates use a neutral color palette but present well due to other well-executed elements. *Between the World and Me* is a clean typographical design and *Autobiography of My Mother* features a lovely illustration on its cover.

Color Theory

Color adds interest and emotion to book covers. According to many color theorists, people can draw 62 to 90 percent of their conclusions about a person or a product based on color, and this is within 90 seconds of meeting them. Readers especially connect to various colors and how a specific color makes them feel. It can affect whether or not they even pick up your book. Choosing the right colors is essential to drawing attention and evoking a positive emotional response. For example, yellow is the color of happiness, optimism, spring and creativity. The cover for *Billion Dollar Lessons* by Paul B. Carroll and Chunka Mui uses a simple bright yellow background, which is suitable given the book's topic. Bright colors grab attention, ignite people and give books an up-beat vibe. Darker blues command strength, reliability and loyalty, while lighter blues signify peace and spirituality.

It's reported that blue is the most liked color in the world for both men and women. One version of Elizabeth Nunez's *Bruised Hibiscus* uses light and deep blues in it's over design. It's cool, tropical and embracing. Warm colors, such as red evoke strong emotions—rage, passion, caution, and adventure. Red drives the cover design of *Sing, Unburied, Sing* by Jesmyn Ward and *Love* by Toni Morrison.

Green symbolizes good fortune, growth, and fertility. Many finance books, such as *Get Good with Money* by Tiffany Aliche, feature green covers, while orange is vibrant, cheerful, youthful, and warm. Colson Whitehead's *The Underground Railroad*, *The Signifying Money* by Henry Louis Gates Jr., and Michael Eric Dyson's *Mercy, Mercy Me* incorporate orange, which is a significant choice considering how uplifting the color orange is in light of the difficult topics covered in those books—tragic and/or triumphant lives.

Purple captures a sense of mystery, magic, and power—think, Dr. Tony Evans' *Our God is Awesome* and Alice Walker's *The Color Purple*. In fact the range of shades in purple communicates various effects. Lighter purples are light-hearted like *The Five Love Languages* by Gary Chapman, while darker purples strike a royal note, representing intelligence and dignity. Pink on the other hand is associated with femininity, fun times, and softness. Maternity books often include pink in its color schemes. Although beige is also a soft color, it is considered more gender neutral and classic. *Never Caught* by Erica Armstrong Dunbar uses beige to complement a powerful retelling of a harrowing journey to freedom.

Black, silver and gold exude wealth and an expensive taste, but black, depending on how it's used, can either give bright colors a boost as in the cover for *Dark Girls* by Bill Duke or drown out your book's vibe. Too much black on a book cover could detract and evoke the wrong mood—drear, sadness, and gloom. But when paired with the right colors or objects, the look and feel hits different—elegant, classy, sure, formal or dramatic. We see this in advertising with luxury car brands like Mercedes—a black Mercedes set in the middle of a gray and black background brings allure not dread.

In contrast, a white cover can disappear online, blending in too much with the white background of Amazon and other book selling Websites. Although white is often chosen as the preferred background color over black due to its neutrality and clean look and feel, beige or cream typically shows better because it doesn't blend into white backgrounds as much. Also, remember to extend the dynamics of your cover scheme to the spine of your book. When your book is on display even in your own home, it will often be displayed upright with only the spine showing, so use colors that will help your book stand out. Take a look at your bookcase today. Which books pop out? What colors are they? Use this insight to help you choose a stand-out spine design.

One additional consideration is the use of brand colors. You can use brand colors for cohesiveness, and it can increase brand recognition. Color is quite impactful. It is what makes your book cover stand out and relay the message you want to deliver. To drive the message home in your head, think about your favorite brand. What color is it? What is the color of a brand you dislike? Think about why you dislike those brands. It could very well be related to the color of the item.

Color Combinations

In addition to choosing the right colors for your book cover, be mindful of color combinations and how those color combinations complement each other. They will add to the book's look and feel. There are all sorts of combinations that play well together. For example, a color combination that includes the primary colors red, yellow and blue are often paired with their compliments. Red's complement is green, purple pairs with yellow, and blue matches orange. Although this is basic color matching, these basics extend into more complicated or relaxed approaches using more sophisticated and complex color schemes.

In the end, you'll want to think about what those color combinations communicate. What does *Some Sing, Some Cry* by Ntozake Shange and Ifa Bayeza communicate? Take a peek at some of the multi-colored covers you pass at the bookstore and note how those covers make you feel—the deep tones, the light tones, the tension and the ease these colors bring to your attention. Then think about your own book cover. Do the color combinations evoke the emotions you want? Do the colors represent the feel and tone of your book? Do the colors blend together well or is it all a bit disjointed? The type of font further enhances the feel of your book.

THE FONT STYLES IN YOUR COVER DESIGN

Your book's title can appear bright and playful or bold and serious using various colors and font combinations. The various font styles include block style, signature, standard type (Roman/Arial/Cambria), and italics. The boldness and large font size of the block style can cover a large area of the page and can be set against a plain background or photograph. Signature font styles are often used for romance titles or historical novels while standard fonts are mixed and matched with others to create a jazzier contemporary vibe. You may want to use fonts similar to those in your branding guide. Pay close attention to how the author's name and other cover elements flow into the cover designs you love, and avoid the word "by" on your cover. A "byline" is reserved for magazines and other publications.

Be sure to choose designers who understand color, image placement and the layering of font styles. Book covers can truly be a work of art. These lessons on color, font, and image placement will help you find the best designer and choose the best cover for you work. Designers are assets, and when you know some of what they know, you can better communicate with them. Tap into this knowledge early on when collaborating and conceptualizing your cover. If you do this, you are more likely to get an outstanding cover that fits your book and your brand.

Hiring Book Designers/Typesetters

When searching for a designer, look for one who has a strong portfolio, preferably a designer who has experience designing different types of books. Many graphic designers may be interested in designing book layouts and covers, but lack the experience necessary to deliver a professional product that meets industry standards. Once you have found a designer, be prepared to ask them a few questions about their design process to decrease the amount of time he or she spends revising over and over. Find out how many changes are allowed once your book has been designed/typeset. Some may allow for minimum change only. One good rule of thumb is to hire a proofreader to go over your manuscript twice. Once before it gets typeset and again after. This is especially important if the copyediting changes were heavy or you only had one round of copyediting. The more revisions you go through after typesetting the more time and money you spend. Most professional book cover and layout designers will create sample covers (per your instructions) for free, but once you go through several designs, they will likely charge you extra for additional samples and revisions.

Giving Interior Design Layout Direction

When preparing your manuscript for interior design, mark your features with design notes. If you are writing a nonfiction book, you will most likely use headings within chapters and sometimes you will have various heading levels. If you are familiar with Website layout design, you know that there are various types of heads marked. H1 is a main title and H2 would be a subhead under the title. They are usually marked using the tags H1, H2, H3, etc. In books, header design follows the same system. Your level one (H1 heads) is the largest font size for main titles. Then come your subheads or H2 heads. If you have more than H1 and H2 heads, let the designer know. Marking your headers will ensure that you receive a more accurate design sample with fewer mistakes. If your designer has to read your whole book to know which header is which, creating your design will end up being time consuming and expensive.

Also, quotes, various types of lists, side bars, poetry, tables, illustrations or diagrams, photos and the like are features designers need to know about head of time. Appearing in some fiction and many nonfiction books, these features are set in a specific design along with the text. So let designers know how many features you have and if you have any preferences. Do you want all the bulleted lists to be designed the same? Do you want borders around features or elements? Should the features have a feminine design? Should the background of the feature include a certain pattern? You don't need to provide any step-by-step instructions per se, but let them know what features are in your book and what, if any, preferences you have. Allow the designer room to create and always request source files of your finished book.

Additional Tips for Working with Book Designers

Select a few favorite covers to share with the designer. Provide a list of covers you like and be sure to list ideal colors—every detail matters. You do want to give your designer creative freedom, but use parameters to ensure you are communicating each aspect of your cover. Let them know if you hate flowers or loathe Roman typeface.

Art, Covers, and Layout Design: Working with Designers

If you want an illustrative cover, avoid copyright infringement by asking the illustrator (which may be a different person) for a collection of styles they can use to create a custom illustration more unique to your book. By doing this you will avoid copying the unique style of a particular artist, which is a copyright violation.

If you have these conversations early on, your sample covers will be closer to what you expect your final cover to resemble. Be upfront about what you want and provide as much information as possible. If you do, you won't need to go through 20 sample cover designs to land a winning cover. Many designers will have intake sheets and a way of collecting information from you upfront, but if they don't, you can still ensure that you and your designers are on the same page by providing your own information.

Chapter 5

Copyright Pages, Publishing Contracts, and Protecting Your Work

Protecting your work isn't necessarily an easy feat. Social media and international interference have created a breeding ground for stealing content. It's even harder to protect an idea that you've shared willy nilly in a conversation or online. Many people think content is unrestricted, but it isn't. Anytime you claim someone's content, and use it in unauthorized ways (like sell it), you are stealing. It can be difficult to determine who has stolen your work, but taking precautions in the beginning will discourage copyright infringement.

Tips for Decreasing Manuscript Theft

❖ Keep ideas about your manuscript to yourself. People share all sorts of information about you without thinking and without your permission, so keep what you say general or don't share at all. This includes Facebook groups, family, friends, influencers, media personalities, and book coaches you don't know.

❋ If you, a project manager, or your publishing coach plan to outsource services to overseas vendors, limit sending early drafts of your manuscript to illustrators, designers, editors, or typesetters. Doing so will cut down on the international distribution of your files before you've had a chance to register your work.

Registration is key. Before your book is published, register your work with the United States Copyright Office. Although your work is protected when you assert ownership and label your material with a copyright notice, unregistered authors face limitations in how much they can gain when suing for infringement. Monetary damages paid to you are much higher if you've registered. It's also important to include the copyright notice on your unpublished manuscript pages. You'd be surprised how many times an unpublished manuscript could change hands unbeknownst to you, the author. Your notice should consist of the word "Copyright" plus the symbol "©" followed by the year of publication and your name or company name. Ultimately, you can't prevent someone from stealing your work, but doing these things can discourage copyright infringement.

When the United States Copyright Office receives your request via the Electronic Copyright Office Registration System, it takes anywhere from one month to seven months to complete.

After you submit your manuscript to the copyright office, you should also obtain a Library of Congress Control Number (LCCN). To begin the process, you will need to create a PrePub Book Link account. If you become a publisher that has published three books by three different authors, you can apply for CIP (Cataloging in Publication) data. Once your account is set up, you can request your LCCN number. To complete the process, you'll need your ISBNs, one for each format (paperback, hardcover, e-book, etc.), your publication or publishing date, and your title page (the title page includes the title and subtitle of your book, your name, and your publishing LLC name and logo). When you receive your LCCN, include it on the copyright page of your book. If you are marketing to libraries, you will need an LCCN number. This is essential if you're working with library vendors, such as Baker & Taylor, Ingram, Innovative Interfaces, etc.

Ownership of Content

When you self-publish you have full ownership (or rather full rights) of your work. The right to publish, license, or distribute belongs to you. When you sign with a publisher, your publishing and distribution rights rest with them. Publishing contracts state the details of your agreement with the publisher. They pay all editorial, production, manufacturing and marketing costs while you accept a grant in lieu of royalties arrangement or an advance—with royalties to follow after the advance is paid back through your book sales. Royalties are usually 10 to 15 percent of your sales. For new traditionally published authors, royalties are around 10 to 12 percent. As dismal as that may sound, if a textbook author, for example, has a book that pulls in 3 million dollars annually, the author will get six figures in royalties, with less legwork involved after the book is written. However, depending on the type of book, the publisher may expect authors to have a large following or audience and expect them to have a marketing plan to promote the book online.

Both publishers and authors contribute to marketing, but the level of participation expected from the author varies from press to press. Fiction writers may be expected to promote extensively, but textbook writers may have the opposite experience. It all depends on the agreement made between author and publisher. Besides some level of promotion by the author, there isn't any additional legwork needed, but if the author is writing a book that will require updating, the author will be expected to revise the book a few years after its release. These book revisions are typically done every 3–4 years on average. However, self-published authors may be able to work more quickly and update annually or quarterly, depending on how quickly updates are needed.

When publishing rights lie with the publisher, some authors may feel that six figures on a book making seven figures is too small, but once you factor in expenses, overhead, paying staff, insurance, revenue losses from books that don't sell, etc., the profit margin isn't always that large. Three million can dwindle quickly, and a self-publishing author doesn't necessarily have the resources that a book publisher has to obtain those numbers. Many older established publishers have deals set up with institutions, universities, book stores and organizations that span decades, even hundreds of years (for example, publisher John Wiley & Sons was founded in 1807). This is why an educator might be perfectly fine with the royalty payments they receive given the exposure publishers can provide. In fact, some books don't earn anywhere near what a publisher is expecting and, as a result, the publisher takes a loss.

Publishing Contracts and Ownership

You should also consider your contract when deciding on traditional publishing. It's important to ask questions and read your contract fully if you decide to commit to a book deal. If you have access to a publishing attorney or an intellectual property attorney, he or she can walk you through everything in your contract. There are pros and cons to both traditional publishing and self-publishing. If you are seeking full control over all aspects of your book, you won't likely get that with a publisher. Corporate decisions are made based on monetary gain—losing money is something a publisher doesn't want. Many good ideas from authors don't necessarily translate into sales and that is what publishers want—reliable sales. If a publisher isn't making money, they will go bankrupt. Their inflexibility is tied to their business sense and financial goals. It's not personal. They want a return on their investment in you. They do not want to risk losing money because they agreed to something simply because you, the author, wanted it done.

Also, think about what you're giving up and discuss those concerns with an intellectual property attorney who specializes in books and publications. There are several sections in a publishing contract authors should pay attention to: grant of rights, warranties and representations, permissions, editing, competing works, royalties and licenses, reversion and termination, and assignment and infringement. Here is a summary of what each term means.

Grant of Rights

The grant of rights part of an author contract gives the publisher exclusive rights to license, print, publish, and/or sell your book in all languages, in all forms (print, digital, audio), in whole or in part, in the United States and all countries of the world. They don't need to ask you for permission to do this, but they will note in your contract if you will receive a percentage from any licensing deals your publisher may make with other entities.

Warranties and Reputations

In this section the author assures the publisher that the manuscript submitted doesn't belong to someone else. The publisher expects you to cite your sources and seek permission before you use any illustrations, photos, or tables that do not belong to you. This is important whether you sign with a publisher or not.

Permissions

Authors are typically responsible for requesting permissions. This includes permission to use any art, song lyrics, or content that doesn't belong to them in their books. Some content doesn't require permission. Public domain (works published before 1926) can generally be used without asking permission. But be sure to check to see if there is a current copyright registration associated with the book that would require seeking permission. For help with permissions, authors can hire a permission editor to help them sort this out. Intellectual property attorneys can also help authors determine if the content falls under "fair use." If permission is needed, some publishers (whether they publish books, music, film, etc.) charge high fees, low fees, or nothing at all. But permission fees are usually paid out of pocket by the author or the publisher could charge it against the book (meaning, the publisher would take it out of the author's advance or royalties). Be prepared to wait anywhere from weeks to months when going through the permissions process.

Editing

This section typically gives details on the editing of your book. When it comes to editing, the author agrees to changes made by the editors. This includes your book title, sub title and other content, such as deleting, adding, or rewording text. If the author doesn't agree, the contract is either terminated or legally enforced. Even though many publishers are flexible in this area, they will take a firm stance on offensive content and racial insensitivity. After the signing of a book contract, the project editor/manager will provide information regarding scheduling and reviewing edits.

Competing Works

This part of the book contract typically states that you, the author, agree not to write and publish a book in your name that would interfere with or decrease the sale or distribution of the book being published. This could be an issue if you have other books you want to write and the publisher isn't interested in publishing them. If those books are seen as competitors, the publisher could sue you for damages or try to discourage or block publication.

Royalties and Licensing

The contract includes details about your royalties, percentages, and how often you will receive them. This includes details surrounding the deals a publisher can make without your permission or on your behalf such as film/TV agreements, licensing deals, and merchandising. Publishers provide details on how frequently you will be paid and who will handle your payment inquiries once your book is published. It isn't uncommon to receive a royalty schedule or calendar from your publisher.

Reversion and Termination

Negotiations can sometimes go south and when that happens the publisher can terminate and revert all rights to you. This part of your contract could also provide information on when rights revert back to you. For example, if your book goes out of print (taken off the market or no longer being printed), you will want to know if the publisher still keeps those rights or if you get those rights back. If you were to pass away, does the publisher keep your book's publishing rights or can you pass them on to your children? Sometimes publishers will hold on to your rights even if they are not actively printing new copies. "Out of print" doesn't automatically mean you get your rights back.

Assignment and Infringement

Under this section, publishers will state the ways in which they can assign or sell your work to another publisher. They will also state their rights and how they may take legal action against you if you infringe on their right to publish your content or assign the publishing of your work to someone else or a publishing partner.

General Rule of Thumb

Be prepared to give up some control and trust the traditional publishing process if you choose it. Ask questions and be aware of the pros and cons. Know the publisher's rights and yours, and seek out a publishing attorney to explain the details of your contract. Decide whether or not it's worth it. Choosing traditional publishing is a personal decision and preferred by many, but an attorney can at least advise you on the law if you'd like additional guidance.

Signing with a publisher can provide you with exposure to other markets and lead you to opportunities for expansion and growth. Plus, their reputation follows you everywhere. In addition, if you get sued or someone tries to steal your content, the publisher is often better positioned to fight. Being a content creator comes with the responsibility of protecting your work, which could be challenging. Registration with the United States Copyright Office gives you documented protection, but fighting people who steal your work is not something everyone is prepared to do. With a publisher, there's usually an attorney on the payroll. But if you have the means, you can hire an intellectual property attorney to help you trademark your work and fight a copyright violator in court. In the end the best decision depends on your goals, your budget, and your reasons for publishing.

Note that there are many advantages on both sides. For many authors ownership of content is paramount because of how they want to use their content in the future. They may want to license their content or negotiate their own partnerships with organizations interested in their work. It all depends on the goals of the author. There is nothing wrong with doing both or choosing one over the other.

What's the Process for Being Published by a Traditional Publisher?

If you are interested in being published by a traditional publisher, you will need to connect to a literary agent or an acquisitions editor. Acquisitions editors are editors who acquire manuscripts and pitch them to publishing executives who manage the purse strings. The pitch is presented with what's called a P&L estimate (profit and loss), which tells the publisher how much it will cost to publish the book, how much money the book is projected to earn and other financials. Acquisitions editors are like the gate keepers to most book deals. They either acquire manuscripts themselves (working directly with the author) or they work solely through literary agents. Larger commercial presses, such as Random House, only use agents and do not accept unsolicited manuscripts.

Literary agents are a bit more accessible than acquisitions editors and they can be found through databases and conferences. Always look for an agent that acquires books in your genre. Take a look at what the agent has acquired and compare your manuscript to others on that list. Also, research which presses the agent acquires for. To meet a literary agent, you would search online through a database or schedule in-person or online meetings with them at a writer's conference. Agents can provide feedback on the strength of your manuscript and make recommendations for improvement, increasing your chances of getting picked up by a reputable publisher. Both literary agents and acquisitions editors travel to writer's conferences and offer opportunities to pitch your query letter or book proposal to them.

In short, query letters and book proposals are what you would use to tell agents and acquisitions editors about you, your book, why you wrote it, and why someone would want to publish or read it. If you've begun working through the master planning discussed in Chapter 1, you already have a great foundation for writing a book proposal or query letter. Also, developmental editors or copy editors with a corporate publishing background can help authors write query letters and proposals, and some are connected to acquisitions editors and literary agents.

Where to Find Literary Agents

- Through a book editor
- Through an online database, such as the Association of Authors' Representatives (AAR), Literary Market Place (LMP), Duotrope, Literary Agents of Color, and Publishers' Marketplace
- While attending certain writers' conferences

When contacting a literary agent online, expect to wait at least a few weeks for a response, and in choosing a publisher, you'll want to properly evaluate them. Just because you're offered a book deal doesn't mean you have to take it. You can also consider hybrid publishers, which are fairly new to the book publishing space. In traditional publishing, you pay zero costs in the publishing of your book, but with hybrid publishers, a fee is charged to help with the cost to publish. They also offer a better royalty percentage. You'll want to understand how the royalty split or advance is determined and (for all presses) find out if they have actual staff or just one person trying to do everything. There are also companies known as vanity presses that offer unfavorable contract terms and high rates to publish your book. Vanity presses can be hard to spot, but knowing the answers to a few questions will help you select the right publisher whether it's a vanity press, a traditional publishing house, or a hybrid arrangement.

TIPS FOR EVALUATING PUBLISHING HOUSES—QUESTIONS TO ASK

- Who owns the rights to your manuscript (distribution, printing, etc.), and how long are you bound to the contract? (When you self-publish, content is owned solely by you, but for traditional publishing and other types, there is a transferring of rights and the details of that are found in the contract.)

Prepping for the Bookshelf

- How many books does this publisher publish per year? (The answer to this question points to the appeal and stability of the press. Reputable publishers publish annually, at least a few titles per year, and there should be at least three to five people on staff who are trained and educated in editing, design, marketing/sales and manufacturing. Poorly staffed publishing houses can be a nightmare.)
- Assess their business procedures. How long have they been in business? What is their workflow and corporate structure? How are decisions made? (New presses could be unstable or have poor business practices. Note whether or not that press has a detailed house style. This lets you know they have real editors who know their craft)
- Note the quality of work. Are the books well published and do they sell? (Pay attention to editing quality, the content, and the book cover design. Check to see if the publisher has books in book stores or libraries.)

If you can do a better job than a traditional publisher, self-publishing is the better choice. But you may also split your efforts and decide to publish your non-fiction through a traditional publisher and self-publish your fiction or vice versa. There are many options and angles. Also keep in mind, traditional publishing is similar to waiting in a long line and waiting your turn. After signing a contract, it will take one to two years, or possibly longer, for your book to be released to the public. Your book is one of many books a publisher will release annually, so be prepared for the process to move slowly.

Chapter 6

The Author Brand: Your Prose is Your Platform

If you want to stand out as an author, attract your ideal readers, and build a thriving author platform, it's important to create a clear and distinct brand that separates you from other authors in your genre. Branding helps you attract new readers, become more recognizable, and build your own community. As mentioned in Chapter 1, branding helps you stand out and it will help inform your marketing and advertising strategy.

Like many authors, you may not know how to build a brand for your author platform. You may feel unsure about what steps to take and what's involved in creating a brand around yourself and your writing. It's not uncommon to think that branding is unnecessary and only for business owners or corporations. Most people are generally familiar with corporate brands and how they influence the masses, but branding also occurs in other areas. Branding in essence is about identifying yourself in a very specific way.

There are many ways a product, service, or person can be branded; two of the most common types are personal and corporate. A personal brand is based on you, as a person—your physical appearance, personality, likes, dislikes, style, philosophy, and beliefs. A corporate brand is typically based on a business that produces a product or service identified primarily through a logo, slogan, and other characteristics—not a person. For example, most people know what the Pepsi logo looks like, but they don't necessarily know who owns Pepsi. Brands driven by a persona include Oprah, Steve Harvey, and others—their faces, names, and personalities stamp all their business endeavors.

Branding for authors follow a similar premise. Your brand is based on what is distinct about you and easily recognized through a collection of identifiers that go beyond fonts and logos. An author brand is a personal brand based on you as an individual. Your writing style, specialty, approach (formal or informal) and your unique abilities all go into your brand. Learning how to use that to grow an audience takes practice and knowledge. In addition, if you already have a business separate from your books, you could use your books to grow your business. But know that if you become someone who publishes your books and others, you are now building a corporate brand and the types of books you publish would drive the image of your company, not you or your face.

Think about the times you've seen companies issue statements regarding people associated with company brands. They'll say, "These views don't accurately reflect the views of our organization," etc. So, consider keeping your books separate from your already established business if you speak on controversial topics. What you say and do will directly impact your business if they are not separate. This can be true for fiction authors who may choose to keep their personal endeavors separate from their company's brand (using a pen name or pseudonym can assist with this as well).

As we look more closely at author branding, we will uncover how an author's book shapes or further defines his or her brand and how that brand will coincide with other endeavors the author may be involved in. There are many possibilities. Authors can even use their books to start new companies. Although authors can approach branding in a number of different ways, we'll first dive deeper into a certain type of branding and explore how you can grow your brand as an author.

What Exactly is an Author Brand?

When it comes to branding, the first object many people think of is a logo, font, or a color palette, but branding is much more than that. It goes far beyond logos, Websites, brand colors and mission statements—even though all of those aspects are a part of branding.

An author's brand is much bigger, and it's all encompassing. It's about who you are as a writer, what you do, and how you present yourself, both online and offline, to your ideal audience.

Your author brand is a personal brand. It is the image you put forth. It's what you stand for. What you're all about—the core of who you are as a person. Essentially, your brand is what makes you unique.

Branding includes your:

- Values
- Unique skills
- Colors and patterns
- Education
- Views or philosophical position
- Novel ideas
- Writing style (spelling, grammar, punctuation style, capitalization style, etc.)
- Experiences
- Stories
- Personality
- Spirituality
- Style or image
- Fonts

Your branding is centered on what you bring to the table and how you appeal to readers. It involves the specific ways you inspire and tell a story and how you address your readers' biggest frustrations or offer solutions. Even though you may struggle to see yourself as a brand at first or think you're too small to even have a brand, think about this:

- If you have an audience, you've already started building a brand.
- Your experiences and thoughts add value.
- If you're communicating your message clearly, your brand is already taking shape.

Authors have the tools to build powerful brands. In fact, you could even say that every person right now is a brand. The question for you is—are you actively growing your brand and controlling how it develops?

There is a Toni Morrison quote that reads: "Your life is already artful—waiting, just waiting, for you to make it art."

That is part of the discovery and ownership process. Your writing life is already full of everything a brand is, and now your creative mind is waiting for you to take hold of it and make it a brand.

Everything you share online, every email you send to your audience, every blog post you write, every live event you host, every podcast—they are all a part of your brand.

They all shape the way people think about you and the image you put forth, but it's always better when you're in control of it. Become aware of all the moving pieces and begin shaping it and molding it—growing into it.

So how do you actively build an author brand? How do you get control of the process? How do you ensure that your brand is helping to build your audience and publishing platform? How do you grow into it? In order to answer those questions, let's first dive into those moving parts and start with the benefits of branding.

THE BENEFITS OF AN AUTHOR BRAND

There are many professionals—entrepreneurs, coaches, consultants, freelancers, etc.—building their brands. You, as an author, should be doing the same.

Building your brand helps grow your author platform. If you are a new author or an author with a small platform, it is important for you to stand out and let your readers know you exist. Like clients and customers, readers are looking for a connection, something recognizable. They are not often drawn to the generic. They are looking for something even when they're not actively searching for it. Readers want dating advice, cooking tips, spiritual guidance, new takes on history, and more. But more than that, it is how YOU give dating advice and the unique ways YOU cook a meal. That is what catches people's attention. Branding benefits authors because it helps readers find you. There are six benefits to building your brand.

1. It allows you to standout from other authors

Your personal values, expertise, and story all set you apart. No one can bring what you bring to the table.

- Insights learned through various experiences (childhood, educational, professional, hobby or travel related)
- Strengths (ability to persuade, compassionate, patient, optimistic, etc.)
- Writing style (humorous, poetic, inclusive tone, etc.)

- Beliefs or philosophies (new spiritual perspectives, or new takes on traditional beliefs)
- Perspectives (political, relational, artistic, modern, etc.)
- Subject of expertise or specialty
- Storytelling skills

These factors set you apart from everyone else. No one else has your unique combination of skills, insights, and experiences.

Building your brand allows you to highlight your uniqueness. It allows you to capitalize on your strengths and the best parts of you. As you highlight your strengths, it distinguishes you from other authors. Think about how Toni Morrison is different from Maya Angelou, how Tananarive Due is different from Octavia Butler, and how June Jordan is different from Bell Hooks. When people shop for their books, they know to expect a certain experience. These authors have become identifiable because their style distinguishes them from others.

The more you work to build your author brand, the more you'll stand out from the crowd.

2. A defined brand allows you to increase your prices

Everything isn't about money, but when you bring a unique voice to the table, you can charge a premium price for other services, such as speaking engagements and workshops.

This happens because books tend to give you more legitimacy in the eyes of your audience—especially if that book is well done. Books are attention grabbers. Through your books you can show off just how different you are. Even if a million authors have written books on a topic you specialize in, such as effective communication, they are not you. You're offering something that can't be found anywhere else. You are the only one who can offer your perspective.

With every piece of content you share, you want to establish yourself as someone who knows how to connect with people. For context, you may also want to research and understand other points of view. Discover the voices of others and decide whether or not you agree and why. Then, form a position. Unique positions can present themselves as invaluable, and the more valuable your content is, the more you will earn trust and establish yourself as an expert.

Charging a higher price for products and services happens when what you're offering is exclusive to you. They can't be purchased at another store or from another person. As you become popular you are bound to attract copycats, which is why protecting your work, as discussed in Chapter 5, is so important. You can even consider trademarking.

The stronger your brand, the more people want your book, your services (if you offer them), and other products. And the more people want your services, the higher the price you can charge.

This is exactly why some speakers are more expensive to book than others. Some authors spent years building their brand into a powerhouse. Readers turn authors into status symbols when the author's quotes and book covers are featured everywhere. They become household names.

You can do what other authors have done—work hard to build your author brand and show how much you bring to the table. Remember, your personal brand is how you present yourself to the world.

3. Developing an author brand puts you in charge of the narrative

As the owner of your brand, you are in charge. And although your personal brand will change and evolve, it all begins with small, seemingly insignificant actions, which you may already be doing. In fact, if you are doing the following, you are already building your personal brand:

- Using social media
- Growing your email list
- Posting on your blog
- Speaking to groups
- Recording and sharing videos

Everything you put out into the world is part of your brand.

- Social media posts
- Newsletters
- Emails
- Videos
- Art or music
- Inspirational graphics or funny memes
- Partnerships with other professionals or organizations
- Meditations
- Affirmations
- Audiobooks
- Podcasts

You're presenting your knowledge and insight to the watching world, proving how you're the go-to person in your genre or specialty. The more expertise you share, the more it shows people that you know exactly what you're talking about.

Once you begin sharing your knowledge, the question becomes: Are you intentionally shaping the narrative of your brand? In other words, are you consciously determining what your brand is all about, or are you letting it happen on a whim at random? Are you thoughtfully curating your brand or are you letting your brand evolve on its own? Are you the one crafting people's opinions about you or are you sort of just letting things happen?

The beauty of branding is that it ensures you're actively shaping your own narrative.

You're determining what others think about you rather than simply letting them form their own opinions. With every social media post you share, every blog post you put up, every email you send, you're shaping the narrative of who you are. You're in control of your story.

4. Branding increases your visibility and footprint

The more you build your brand, the more visible you'll become.

- You'll attract more fans on social media.
- Those fans will share your content with their inner circle.
- You'll begin forming your own community.

It's a powerful cycle.

As your fan base grows, you can expect to be featured in the media—newspapers, magazines, TV segments, Instagram lives, and more.

Media outlets are always looking for experts to comment on particular subjects, and when you become known as the expert in your field or mastering the art of telling a certain type of story, you'll start generating media requests. The more you're featured in the media, the more opportunities you'll have to speak in front of people. Conference organizers are always looking for well-known personalities to speak.

Building your brand as an author and building your platform go hand-in-hand. As your brand grows stronger, your platform will get bigger, which will then make your brand stronger. The stronger your brand the more likely your fan base will grow even more. As you become more visible, it is even more important to pay attention to how consistent you are in the types of content you share.

5. Your author branding shapes the content you share

As an author, you'll want to solidify your author branding by putting together a set of guidelines. These guidelines will ensure consistency, and they can also include many of the standard guideline elements businesses use, such as font style, colors and the correct and incorrect ways to use a particular logo (if applicable). Having author-branding guidelines for the content you share is an important step in growing into your brand.

When you don't have guidelines, you end up sharing either nothing at all or whatever catches your fancy at any given moment. Neither of these strategies contribute to your brand as an author. Your brand guidelines direct you toward sharing relevant content. Here are the types of information you should consider including in your guidelines:

- Range of Subjects—the types of topics you discuss
- Type of Content—inspiration, how-to, tips, strategies, reviews, etc.
- Quotes or Sayings—affirmations, quotes and sayings from you, not others
- Editorial Style Preferences—unique spellings, words to avoid, grammar preferences

You should only share content that aligns with and promotes the values of your author brand. It's tempting to post a random meme that has nothing to do with your brand. It might be funny, but if it doesn't add to your brand, it could detract from your brand. Post a meme related to your brand instead.

6. Strong author branding allows you to become a genre influencer

The more you develop your author brand the more you become known as a genre influencer—someone who significantly shapes the opinions of their readers and has a big influence on how they react to other books, products, views, and what they purchase.

There are some significant benefits to being an influencer:

- You'll sell more books.
- Publishing companies and organizations will want to partner with you, which can result in you earning more revenue.
- You can license your content just like large publishing companies do.

The Power of a Strong Author Brand

The more you focus on your own brand, the more visible you become and the more you become known as an expert. Your writing can stand out in how you:

- Create gripping plots or cliff-hangers
- Fold metaphor, symbolism, allegory, or other literary elements into your stories
- Create complex or memorable characters
- Tackle taboo subjects
- Present new research or data
- Bring light to an unknown event or condition
- Explain difficult concepts in creative ways
- Use humor, satire, or word pictures

The more you're known as an expert in some way, the more you will receive recognition. Brand building is a door opener.

CHAPTER 7

How to Develop and Grow Your Author Brand

"The most efficient, most productive, most useful aspect of branding is creating a new category. In other words, narrowing the focus to nothing and starting something new."

–Al Ries and Laura Ries,
The 22 Immutable Laws of Branding

Author branding may sound fancy and intimidating, but the key to settling into your brand identity is simplicity and authenticity. Be authentic about who you are now as an author. Your brand will grow and change as you do, but focus on who you are now. It's tempting to idolize and emulate other powerful well-known authors, but a strong brand must be built around you and not anyone else. When you start with yourself, you will discover your uniqueness, which will lead to developing a prose style and an identity different from other authors. Let's break this down further using a nine-step process.

Step #1: Who are you?

The first step is to determine who you are. This step is built on your writing style, skills, experience, passions, values, and beliefs. You must know yourself if you want to build a strong brand.

Questions to ask yourself:

- What kind of writer am I?
- How am I different from my favorite writers?
- Is my writing style more structured or free form?
- Am I comfortable writing in active voice or the more formal passive voice?
- What unique skills do I have?
- What are my core values?
- What am I most passionate about?
- What unique experiences have shaped who I am?
- What knowledge do I have to offer that no one else does?

The answers to these questions help shape your brand. They will help you get to the core of what matters most to you and how you connect to your audience.

Step #2: Determine what you want to accomplish

Once you've identified the core of who you are, think about what you want to accomplish. Ponder these questions:

- What would I like to accomplish as an indie author?
- What do I want to be known for?
- If I could be the world's foremost expert on a topic, what would it be?
- What story themes do I want to be known for?
- What key messages do I want to communicate?
- If I could only give one piece of advice, what would it be?

The answers to these questions should further solidify in your mind what your author brand will look like.

Step #3: Identify your target audience

As we mentioned in Chapter 1, a broad audience is not a target audience. You can't effectively serve everyone. Rather, there is a core demographic of people who will resonate deeply with you and appreciate what you are writing about and how you are writing about it.

This core demographic is your target audience. These are the people you will serve most effectively. They will be your ideal readers.

To identify your core audience, ask yourself these questions:

- What does my reader want?
- What is the reading level of my reader?
- Is my reader an adult or a child?
- How can I help readers?
- Who will benefit most from my skill set and knowledge?
- Who am I most passionate about serving?
- Who will resonate most with my brand and me?
- Is my reader strictly a read-write learner, an audio-visual person, a hands-on learner, or a different type?

If you are a fiction author, ask yourself these questions:

- Do my readers like cliffhangers?
- Do my readers like sequels?
- Do they enjoy complex characters or plots?
- Is a happy ending a must for my reader?
- Does my reader desire a story without loose ends?

- Does my reader enjoy long layered stories or shorter fiction?
- Does my reader like twists and turns?
- How old is my reader and where is my reader from (what city, region or country)?

When determining your core audience, create a specific portrait of your reader. This portrait represents your ideal reader. Include the following information in your portrait:

❀ Demographics: How old are they? Man? Woman? Single? Married? Race? There are many more identifiers within gender, sexuality, and culture you can determine along with your reader's education level. Also, note their careers. How much do they make? Where do they live? Are they spiritual? Do they go to church? What kind of church?
❀ Hopes and dreams: What do they want their future to look like? What are their goals?
❀ Challenges: What obstacles do they face? Why haven't they been able to reach their goals? What do they want your book to do for them?

Step #4: Determine your powerful prose position

Your powerful prose position (PPP) is your unique writing expression, your unique artistic value. A PPP pinpoints how your writing style and content are unique and how you are positioned to influence and empower readers. It is powerful because it is unique. It is your brand summed up into a single, compelling statement that describes exactly what kind of author you are and how you will impact readers.

It's where you take all the answers from the previous three points and put them together into one brand statement that sums up who you are and how you serve your core audience.

Here's an example:

I use my writing (style + genre) to (achieve X) so that readers can (outcome)

So your powerful prose position may be something like, "Using my sense of humor, I write to inspire budget-conscious single moms to declutter, organize and free themselves from stuff so they may live a freer more fulfilled life."

Below are some other PPP examples:

"I created my own theories and strategies to provide content for creative entrepreneurs who want to scale their businesses to over six-figures per year."

"I prepare elementary-aged children for reading and understanding word problems by sharing my own method through picture books."

"My style of fiction uses metaphor and allegory to tell the stories of women who have overcome racial workplace trauma to build export/import businesses."

Your powerful prose position (PPP) doesn't have to say everything about your brand, but it should get right to the heart of who you are and how you will help or inspire your audience.

It may help to give your PPP a name that will stick in people's minds. For example, if you teach gospel singers how to be more productive, you could call your PPP the "Productive Praise Formula."

Or if you write books to help fundraising entrepreneurs scale their businesses on a shoestring budget, you could call your powerful prose name something like, "Pennies to Profit."

It simply needs to be short, memorable, and aptly describe what you do.

Avoid skimping on this step. Creating your powerful prose position gives you a high degree of clarity about what your brand is all about. It positions you in a way that helps you stand out from the crowd.

Step #5: Brand yourself and build a brand strategy

Once you've identified the core of your brand and determined your target audience, you can work on building infrastructure and designs that communicate your message visually. Create a traditional marketing branding guide that includes fonts, colors, and possibly a logo. In every communication with your audience, whether it's a blog post, email, podcast, social media post, etc., stay true to your brand message. Your social media banners and email headings should reflect your brand. The design should be consistent across all platforms. Consider using the same one or two professional photos of yourself. How you are styled in these photos will reflect your brand—consider wearing or accessorizing using your brand colors. If you're not sure about your brand's colors, go neutral with nudes, whites, blacks and tans so that it is easier to transition into brand-specific colors.

Also consider the overall feel of your brand. Is it soulful, hippie, classic, eclectic, modern, formal, eco-chic, militant, Afrocentric, or youthful? For example, if your brand is luxurious, your styling would be formal—suit or heels, classy jewelry, etc.

Your message should constantly speak about the problems you solve, the clarity you bring, the inspiration you deliver, the value you offer, or the level of entertainment you can provide. Constantly encourage your audience; consistently voice the message of your brand.

Just like horror fiction author Stephen King wouldn't likely start writing romance or become an authority on the romance novel, don't switch from a genre you know to something else out of the blue. Is it likely for Danielle Steele to release a sci-fi novel under her name? Established authors are actively writing in the genre that best represents them. This strengthens their brand identity as authors. And readers expect consistency, a clear identity. If readers find that you're not producing what they love, they will move away from you. Huge leaps away from your genre should only be done if you are rebranding yourself or if you're a genre-bending author who wants to write in various genres. If that is you and you want a strong brand with a writing portfolio that includes experimental fiction, horror, romance and even a nonfiction how-to book, choose a common theme or subject for all of them (for example, every book you write features singers, and your how-to is a singing manual). In this case a common theme or element ties everything together. Your brand becomes one based on subject, theme, or character type instead of genre. It's perfectly fine to rebrand or reinvent yourself, but once you settle into your brand, it's better to settle in.

Try to avoid randomly going off brand in your communications. Everything you write or share on social media or elsewhere should reinforce your powerful prose position. Remind yourself of what you want to be known for. Much of Toni Morrison's fiction centers on a woman lead character facing severe hardship. Walter Mosley focuses on male Black heroes. That is what they're known for. If you find that your brand isn't as succinct as these prominent authors, maybe you haven't spent enough time developing your gifts and talents and tapping into your unique experience. You may not know who you are yet or what you bring to the table. When you discover this, you will naturally fall into your genre, and settle deep enough into it to build a strong brand. As you grow, your powerful prose position will impact your communication and your messaging.

Authentic messaging flows into creating a strong, compelling Website or Facebook or some other fan page, which will serve as your home base for all your online activities. Online you should portray yourself as a strong, compelling brand, not an insignificant one. Encourage yourself and treat yourself as you are: a powerful brand that isn't ordinary and generic. Remember in Chapter 1 when we discussed competition and similar titles? When you determine your PPP, you'll notice where you fall more easily and you'll recognize your value. You start to realize that you are a part of a whole and that there is a unique spot just for you.

It is also worth noting that branding is something you can scale up or down. A fiction author may not need a logo or all the bells and whistles of traditional branding. They might focus more on the genre of books they publish and the content they share online. A nonfiction author will more likely have a business or a need for an extensive branding guide and logo. Since many authors have crossed over from fiction to non-fiction and vice versa, it is a good idea to practice good brand management and become aware of how branding helps build platforms. A confusing brand with too much going on can take away from the strength of your platform. Separating brands may be necessary in this case.

Step #6: Create Your Website

Your online presence should match your brand. Whether it's your Website, YouTube channel or some other social media page, you need a space online that will function as your home base. It will be one of the primary places people will go to find out who you are and what you do.

Your home base is one of the primary ways you turn visitors into readers.

First impressions are important. Visitors should immediately determine how interesting your books are. If they see a poorly done cover, missing book descriptions, or typos everywhere, there's a good chance they'll become disinterested.

So how do you ensure that your home base stands out to readers?

- Display your books. They should have professionally designed covers. Professional covers are sometimes inexpensive if you shop around, so there's little excuse for having a poorly done cover. A bad cover reflects poorly on you as an author.
- As mentioned earlier, determine your brand colors, font and editorial style—which would include how you approach word choice, punctuation, and voice (first person, third person, passive, active, etc.) This should be reflected in your Website design and copy.

Ideally, your powerful prose position will be front and center, the first thing that people see. It should be impossible to miss. It should function like the main headline in a newspaper. The eye should be drawn to it immediately. You should also:

- Use professional photographs. Hire a professional photographer or consult with one. Low-quality photos will reflect poorly on your brand.
- Use reader reviews and endorsements. They help overcome your prospects hesitation and objections. Also, if you've been featured in any media outlets, show off those credentials too.
- Present a clear call-to-action to buy your book or do something. Ultimately, you want people to take action when they're on your Website or home base. You want them to buy your book, watch your interview, or enter an autographed book giveaway. Give visitors a clear call-to-action.
- Create a compelling About page. In your About section, tell your story. How did you get to where you currently are? What motivates you to serve your audience? Why do you do what you do? If you are a fiction writer, what are the common themes you write about?
- If you offer services, create a services page. It's important to have a clear services page that explains what you offer, what's included, and more.
- Give away free resources, a guide, a template, a master class, a free chapter, etc. Consider printing special editions of your book for a giveaway, such as an autographed hardcover edition with specialty fabric or a fancy embroidered paper book jacket. Make it standout. Let it show off your personality.

✺ Create a contact page. Obviously, you want a way for people to be in touch with you. You can use the contact page on your Website or accept direct messages through social media.

Step #7: Develop your content strategy

Another way to build your brand is to create strategic content. As mentioned before, once you've determined your brand, it's important to start treating yourself as a brand.

There are two paths you can take to develop content. One approach is to follow current trends in your genre, which is how publishers often strategize. They study the market and base their approaches on what is likely to be well received. The second way is based on you being the first to do something. This approach is often an "away from the pack" approach. It's similar to how Toni Morrison came into the author life, "If there is nothing out there like what you want to read, you must write it."

In the book *The 22 Immutable Laws of Branding* being the first means that you set the trends and eventually others begin to copy and pattern themselves after you. Of course, you have to be prepared for your approach to go the other way, which means it may not catch on. You may lose money, and your approach falls into obscurity. This is why many publishing companies decide on growing or acquiring market share in an established moneymaking market instead of an out-of-the-box new idea.

Whether you choose to approach branding using the "in the current market" strategy or the "be the first" strategy, you will need to develop an on-message content strategy where your content reinforces some or part of your brand. Maybe one day you speak to a particular pain point for readers. On another day you encourage your audience to strive for their goals. Whatever the case, it's essential that your content ties into your brand.

- Publish your content on your primary platform, whether that's your blog, YouTube, podcast, etc.

Write your content ahead of time, then break it down into smaller, shareable pieces of content. In other words, if you have a 10-minute video, find three parts of that video that could be shared on their own and extract those clips.

If you have a 1,000-word blog post, extract five 100-word excerpts that can stand on their own.

- Share the smaller pieces of content across all your channels. Once you've created your smaller pieces of content, you're going to post those across all your channels, including Facebook, Instagram, LinkedIn, Twitter, email, etc.
- Repeat the process again and again. By consistently sharing your brand message, you'll steadily build your audience.

By writing your content ahead of time, you ensure that every piece of content you post is always brand related. Planned content is more likely to be on message than impromptu content. Your Facebook posts, Instagram videos, blog posts, YouTube videos, and emails are always speaking your brand message to your audience.

You can also repurpose content into different formats. For example, if you have unreleased book content that didn't make it into your final manuscript, you could turn that into a guide, a workbook, or a series of blog posts. The only pitfall to watch out for is having too much unrelated content under one brand and not separating. If your brand is politics and public service but you love to cook, consider another entity or channel under your cooking brand. But keep in mind that creating too many brands could weaken your original brand.

Step #8: Consistently add value important to your audience

When it comes to building your brand, it's essential that you share valuable content with your audience without asking for anything in return. Yes, there will be times when you invite people to buy your book, but you want to encourage connection and conversation. The main take away for readers when they interact with you is how much inspiration or value you provide.

You want to give your audience tips, tools, and the useful content they've been wanting—unpublished content presented to them in different ways. A winning content strategy taps into the needs of your target audience. Are they into arts and crafts? Do they keep up with certain current events? How is that affecting your readers? Always keep yourself in touch and relevant to what's going on locally or nationally. Content should be timely and in tune with what's current and what you're passionate about. If you don't put out fresh, relevant content, you risk losing people over time.

Step #9: Build a community

One of the best ways to build your author brand is to build a community where you and your readers can all help or inspire each other. The value in building a community around your brand is that it gets others involved in helping to promote your brand and uplift others.

Create a squad or group of passionate people who care about the same things you do. Some simple ways to build a community include:

- Starting a private Facebook group or an online class. In this group, people can interact with each other, share ideas, interact with you, raise questions, etc.
- Starting a membership/subscription. With memberships, you can share exclusive content slowly over a period of time. Your memberships can

be free or tiered. You can offer additional digital products (checklists, guides, toolkits, courses, master classes, workshops) as a part of a premium membership where your readers are paying a monthly subscription for access.
- Hosting live events. Live events allow you to meet your readers in real time. Live webinars, virtual conferences, online workshops, and talks are all great ways to deepen your relationships with them. Consider pre-recorded master classes, masterminds, and retreats as well.
- Creating a transformative coaching program. If you are an author who is also a coach, you can give people exclusive access to you and the coaching you provide. Teach them to unlock their inner poet or use your stories to help them overcome challenges. You can also give them access to things like group or one-on-one calls every month, ongoing webinars, and a forum where they can interact with you and other trainees.
- Creating an online magazine featuring articles from you, your team, or your readers. This creates community and gives readers something they will look forward to because they are a part of it.
- Creating a crafting community using your words to create art—collages, book-binding projects, jewelry, altered books, or art journals.

As you build or reinvent your brand, remember what we covered:

- Identify who you are and what matters to you.
- Define your core audience.
- Determine your powerful prose position (PPP).
- Treat yourself like a brand.
- Create your compelling Website or home base.
- Create your content strategy.
- Constantly bring your best self to your audience.
- Build your community.

The more you do those things, the more you'll attract your ideal readers. Your author platform can serve as a springboard to many other endeavors, and strong branding can help you build and grow.

Conclusion

The indie publishing landscape can be daunting at times. There are so many self-published authors doing so many different things in so many different ways. It can be hard to know which path is the right path. You'll ask yourself: What type of book should I share with the world? What do I want to say? How do I reach my audience? Getting from point A to point B can be draining, but the tips shared in this book are meant to help you create an indie publishing process that is a soul-enriching journey—an empire you will rule and control.

But whether you adopt some of these methods and strategies or all of them, I hope you are now better able to adapt to whatever comes your way as an indie author. The path to self-publishing does not have to be an impossible or spirit-draining task. It can be the most empowering thing you've ever done. Putting your work out there for the world to read is an amazing accomplishment. Just know; you can "do" self-publishing, and you are well on your way to not only writing one book, but many books, and publishing them well.

References

Dzulkifli, Mariam A. and Mustafar, Muhammad Faiz, "The Influence of Colour on Memory Performance: A Review," *Malaysia Journal of Medical Science*, 20, no. 2 (March 2013): 3–9.

Jonauskaite, Domicele, Mohr, Christine, Antonietti, Jean-Philippe, Spiers, Peter M., Althaus, Betty, Anil, Selin, and Dael, Nele, "Most and Least Preferred Colours Differ According to Object Context: New Insights from an Unrestricted Colour Range," *PLoS One*, 11, no. 3 (2016).

Boddy-Evans, Marion, "The Spruce Crafts What Are Complementary Colors? What Are Complementary Colors? Learn How to Use Complementary Paint Colors to Your Advantage," *The Spruce Crafts*, October 31, 2019.

Six Degrees. "International Color Symbolism Chart," accessed September 9, 2021, https://www.six-degrees.com/pdf/International-Color-Symbolism-Chart.pdf

UNICEF. "Babies need humans, not screens: Find out why, and how, too much screen time can harm your child," unicef.org

Pappas, Stephanie, "What Do We Really Know about Kids and Screens?" APA, 51, no. 3 (April 1, 2020).

Dzulkifli, Mariam A. and Mustafar, Muhammad Faiz, "The Influence of Colour on Memory Performance: A Review," *Malaysia Journal of Medical Science,* 20, no. 2 (March 2013): 3–9.

Jonauskaite, Domicele, Mohr, Christine, Antonietti, Jean-Philippe, Spiers, Peter M., Althaus, Betty, Anil, Selin, and Dael, Nele, "Most and Least Preferred Colours Differ According to Object Context: New Insights from an Unrestricted Colour Range," *PLoS One,* 11, no. 3 (2016).

Boddy-Evans, Marion, "The Spruce Crafts What Are Complementary Colors? What Are Complementary Colors? Learn How to Use Complementary Paint Colors to Your Advantage," *The Spruce Crafts,* October 31, 2019.

Six Degrees. "International Color Symbolism Chart," accessed September 9, 2021, https://www.six-degrees.com/pdf/International-Color-Symbolism-Chart.pdf

UNICEF. "Babies need humans, not screens: Find out why, and how, too much screen time can harm your child," unicef.org

Pappas, Stephanie, "What Do We Really Know about Kids and Screens?" *APA,* 51, no. 3 (April 1, 2020).

Pappas, Stephanie, "What Do We Really Know about Kids and Screens?" *APA,* 51, no. 3 (April 1, 2020).

Perrin, Andrew, "One-in-Five Americans Now Listen to Audiobooks," *Pew Research Center,* September 25, 2019.

Ries, Al and Ries, Laura. 1998. The 22 Immutable Laws of Branding: *How to Build a Product or Service into a World-Class Brand.* New York: HarperCollins Publishers.

Osterwalder, Alexander and Pigneur, Yves. 2010. *Business Model Generation: A Handbook for Visionaries, Game Changers, and Challengers.* New Jersey: John Wiley & Sons.

Fishman, Stephen. 2020. *The Copyright Handbook: What Every Writer Needs to Know*, 14th Edition. California: Nolo.

Booth, C. Wayne, Colomb, Gregory G., Williams, Joseph M., Bizup, Joseph and Fitzgerald, William T. 2016. T*he Craft of Research, 4th Edition.* Chicago: The University of Chicago Press.

Appendix A

Questions to Ask Creative Professionals

Questions for Beta Readers and Peer Reviewers

NONFICTION

Is my title and subtitle a good fit for my book?

Was my book hard to read?

What themes did you recognize in my book?

Were my metaphors and analogies clear and understandable?

Did you have any questions about the terms I defined in my book?

Were my definitions clear or should I elaborate and give more detail?

Do you think my table of contents is complete? Should I add more chapters?

Appendix A - Questions to Ask Creative Professionals

If my table of contents was not complete, what chapters should I add?

If someone asked you what my book was about, what would you say?

Could you tell, based on the content, who my audience is?

How would you describe my writing style? Laid-back, formal, long-winded, complicated, descriptive, or to-the-point?

What type of writing do you prefer (academic, casual, funny, etc.)?

Did you need to read any of my sentences more than once to understand what I was trying to say?

Did you think the statements made in my book were reasonable or accurate?

How long did it take you to read my book?

Was my book a quick read, an average read or a long read?

Does my book come across as preachy?

How did you feel after reading my book? Happy, depressed, encouraged, inspired, comforted, hopeful, angry, or motivated?

Were my chapters well organized or did you get lost or confused while reading?

Which parts confused you? List page numbers.

If you could describe my book in three words, which words would you choose?

Prepping for the Bookshelf

Which chapter was your favorite and why?

What was your least favorite chapter and why?

Is this a book you would buy? Why or why not?

Can you think of three people who would enjoy reading my book?

What did you learn after reading my book?

Could you teach what I shared to someone else?

Is there anything missing?

Did you find that my book was too similar to someone else's?

How many ah-ha moments did you have while reading my book? What were they?

If you could change one thing about my book, what would it be?

Was my book too short or too long?

Does my book need major revisions? If so, what should I consider?

Did you like my book?

Would you read it again?

FICTION

Who is your favorite fiction author?

If someone asked you to describe the setting of my story, could you picture where my story took place?

Could you follow the dialogue at all times? Did you know who was speaking?

Did you always know what was happening?

Were my flashbacks confusing?

Did I use too much vernacular or not enough?

Did I use too much profanity?

Who was your favorite character?

Who was your least favorite character?

Which character was most relatable?

How would you describe my characters? Stupid, naïve, smart, creative, ruthless, violent, kind, funny, serious, laid-back?

Did you relate to my protagonist?

Did you relate to my antagonist?

Were my characters believable?

Were my character descriptions vivid? Could you imagine them?

Was there a character you loved to hate? Why?

Was there a character that you didn't care about?

Were my characters too flat?

Was my sub-plot confusing?

Would my story read better if it was written in the first person or third person?

Could you keep track of each character and the role they played in my story?

How did you feel after you read my story? Happy, sad, frustrated, disappointed, satisfied, or angry?

Did you read any parts that made you uncomfortable?

Did any of my content offend you?

What lessons were illustrated in my story?

Were there any parts that moved too slowly?

Did you find a plot hole?

Did I tell more than show?

Appendix A - Questions to Ask Creative Professionals

Is my book balanced? Did you find that I needed more of one thing and less of something else?

How long did it take you to read my book?

Were there any parts that left you hanging or did anything feel unresolved?

Did any of my characters do anything out of the ordinary that surprised you? Did you like this? Why or why not?

Did my story represent historical or current events well?

Did you recognize any of the symbolism in my story?

Did you like the ending?

Was the ending too abrupt?

Was the ending satisfying?

Was my story similar to other stories you've read? If so, in which books?

Did you think my story should have a sequel?

Should I rewrite this story as a screenplay?

Would you recommend my story to others?

Is this a book you would buy?

Questions to Ask Editors

Which style guide do you use?

Do you have a house style?

Where did you learn how to edit?

What is your level of education? Do you have an English degree, certification, certificate, or apprenticeship?

How much do you charge for an editing sample?

Are you comfortable using an editorial style sheet?

In what format should I submit my manuscript? Word, Google Docs, PDF?

To edit, do you use Tracked Changes in Word?

Do you recommend editing software like Grammarly or Pro Writing Aid?

Is your style of editing usually light, medium, or heavy?

Describe your editorial process? How do you approach editing?

Do you work with authors seeking to be signed to a traditional publishing house?

Appendix A - Questions to Ask Creative Professionals

Do you assist with pitching to agents and acquisitions editors?

Can you help me with my query letter or proposal?

Can you refer me to a publicist?

Do you know anything about marketing, book launches, or social media?

Can you help me with my bio or my back cover copy?

Can I put you on retainer? If so, what does that look like?

Are you a developmental editor, a copy editor, a line editor, or a proofreader? How do you define each type?

Can you help me analyze my reviewer or beta reader data?

If I am requesting copyediting, how many rounds of editing are included per service? Do I get one review or do you check my work again after I have reviewed your edits and made changes?

How long will it take for you to edit my work?

What should my expectations be when working with an editor? Will you catch every error?

Can you check my references/endnotes/bibliography?

Can you recommend book layout designers, cover designers, indexers, and book marketers?

Can I list your name in the Acknowledgements section of my book?

Can you research topics in my book for me?

Can you help me write my book?

Can you help me find art or an illustrator?

Do your agreements have a confidentiality clause?

Can I hire you as a contributor or co-author?

How many editors should I have?

Do you outsource any editing overseas?

Can you serve as my project manager and handle the entire process for me?

Can I find books you edited at the bookstore?

What topics do you specialize in?

Do you specialize in a specific genre?

How did you decide on a specialty?

If you specialize in fiction, what type? Romance, African American Fiction, Mystery, Science Fiction, Literary, etc.?

If you specialize in literary fiction, which literary theories do you gravitate toward?

What do you love about editing?

Have you written your own books? Why or why not?

Appendix A - Questions to Ask Creative Professionals

How long have you been editing?

What are your office hours?

Can I text you?

Can you coach me?

Can I buy coaching sessions in bulk (three to five sessions at a time)?

Do you communicate primarily through email, phone, or Zoom?

How often will I hear from you during this process? Once per week, a few times per week or at the start and the end of the process?

Can you help me develop my outline?

Can you help me develop my characters?

How do you price your services? What is included? How many rounds of editing? How many hours of coaching?

Do you work with students?

Who is your ideal client?

What is the average word count of most books you edit?

Can you help me request permissions?

How far in advance can I schedule your services?

Do you offer payment plans?

Do you offer guarantees?

Can you advise me on best practices and the ins and outs of book publishing?

Do you work with writers whose second language is English?

What is your cancellation policy?

Do you offer refunds?

What if I don't like the editing?

Can you recommend a writer's group, a book, or a class to help me become a better writer?

Are your contracts online or will I need to print, scan, and email back?

I need reminders. Can you send me reminders or updates during the process?

QUESTIONS TO ASK COVER/INTERIOR LAYOUT BOOK DESIGNERS OR TYPESETTERS/FORMATTERS

How many bound print books have you designed?

How long does it take to layout a 200-page (or larger) book?

Do you design in InDesign, Quark, or a different program?

Appendix A - Questions to Ask Creative Professionals

Have you ever worked for a publisher or designed an award-winning cover?

What is your process for designing? Is there an intake form?

Can I send you the title of a book that has a layout I like?

Can I choose the font size?

What size margins do you recommend?

What will the spacing be in between the lines of text?

Can you recommend the best trim size for my genre?

Can I have the source files when completed?

How many interior samples do I get to choose from?

How many book spine designs do I get to choose from?

Do you design interior layout and covers?

How many cover design samples do I get to choose from?

Can you help me find photos or an illustrator?

Can you help me choose a binding?

Do you work with one-column, two-column, or three-column designs?

Do you have a preferred or recommended printer?

Prepping for the Bookshelf

After proofreading, how many changes do you allow before charging extra?

Can you help me upload files to Amazon, Ingram Spark, or a small independent printer?

If I find a mistake after my book is published, how much will you charge for corrections?

Are you well versed in color theory or color psychology?

Have any of your covers sold thousands of copies?

Do you mainly design adult fiction, children's books, or non-fiction?

Do you have experience laying out books that have photos? How many photos on average?

Appendix B

The Publishing Readiness Checklist

Editorial

- ☐ Development check complete
    - ☐ All concepts thoroughly explained
    - ☐ Accuracy and references checked
    - ☐ Target audience confirmed
    - ☐ Chapters follow logical order
    - ☐ Reader/reviewer feedback incorporated
- ☐ Completed front matter
    - ☐ Introduction or Preface
    - ☐ Dedication
    - ☐ Acknowledgements
    - ☐ Finalized table of contents
    - ☐ Copyright page
- ☐ Copyediting complete
    - ☐ Finalized title and table of contents
- ☐ Permissions acquired if needed
- ☐ Page count estimate completed
- ☐ Back mater completed
    - ☐ Index
    - ☐ Appendices
    - ☐ Advertising (if allowed, some distributors don't allow this)

Production

- ☐ Finalized page count
- ☐ Added page numbers to table of contents
- ☐ Completed page numbering and updated table of contents
- ☐ Proofing complete
- ☐ Cover (Front, Back, Spine)
    - ☐ Interior layout design approved
    - ☐ Front and back cover design approved
    - ☐ Inside cover copy completed
- ☐ Back cover copy completed (bio, book summary, quotes from endorsers or reviewers, IBSN, barcode, price)
- ☐ Determine your distributor: Ingram Spark, Amazon, Apple Books

Social Media Strategy

- ☐ Amazon or Bookshop Ads
    - ☐ Set budget
    - ☐ Set ad duration
    - ☐ Determine keywords to be used
    - ☐ Completed ad copy and design
- ☐ Facebook Ads
    - ☐ Type of media selected (video or photo)
    - ☐ Ad type selected (traffic, lead, conversion, messenger, etc.)
    - ☐ Custom audience set
    - ☐ Determined budget per day
    - ☐ Set length of time
    - ☐ Created ad copy
- ☐ Pinterest Ads
    - ☐ Pinned to a blog that discusses your book
    - ☐ Compiled a list of keywords
    - ☐ Created video or story pins
    - ☐ Determined budget per day

- ❏ Set length of time
- ❏ YouTube
    - ❏ Created a YouTube Channel
    - ❏ Vlogged about your book
    - ❏ Posted an author interview
    - ❏ Designed a book trailer for YouTube ads and other social media platforms
- ❏ Email Marketing
    - ❏ Shared related topics that point readers to your book
    - ❏ Shared book release date
    - ❏ Selected book excerpts to share
- ❏ Chose vendor to automate content (Mailchimp, Active Campaign, Flodesk, Constant Contact, etc.)
- ❏ Twitter
    - ❏ Updated your cover with your book's release date
    - ❏ Tweeted lines from your book and tweet links to your blog
- ❏ Publicity
- ❏ Create a list of media outlets you can pitch to—TV, social media influencers, podcast hosts
- ❏ Instagram
- ❏ Design graphics using lines from your book.
- ❏ Posted the book cover for a cover release post.
- ❏ Posted images related to the content you cover
- ❏ Posted images from your book
- ❏ Engaged with your followers, asking them questions, asking them for feedback (e.g., "Help me choose the cover for my next book." And list potential covers)
- ❏ Podcast
- ❏ Created a podcast or created a list of podcasts where you can appear as a guest
- ❏ Author Website
    - ❏ Bio/About completed
- ❏ High-resolution photos and book cover uploaded
- ❏ Reviews/testimonials/endorsements received and uploaded

- ☐ Services (if any) listed
- ☐ Call to action (buy, read, sign up) included
- ☐ Video (book summary, interview, or book trailer) uploaded
- ☐ Link included for purchasing your book
- ☐ Free sample chapter or book giveaway offered
- ☐ Contact page and links to social media and podcasts included
- ☐ Blog or podcast created
- ☐ SEO Strategy
  - ☐ Created an SEO strategy to include keywords and relevant search questions.

General Marketing

- ☐ Reviews are in from various outlets, book journalists, and bookstagrammers on Instagram, Pinterest, or Twitter.
- ☐ Finalized number of comp (free) signed copies for book reviewers, giveaways, editors and influencers
- ☐ Connected with local book stores to pitch your books, schedule interviews, or set up virtual or in-person events.
  - ☐ Pitched to local or national book clubs and book boxes
  - ☐ Set up for direct mail campaigns completed
  - ☐ Completed advertorial
  - ☐ Sent enlarged post card

Appendix C

Chapter Development Worksheet

Chapter Title:

Chapter Objectives:

Chapter Summary:

Appendix C - Chapter Development Worksheet

Creating Content for Chapters:

What is your main subject?

List all related topics:

Topic 1

Topic 2

Topic 3

Prepping for the Bookshelf

Research Topics and Collect Information:

People I need to interview:

Books I need to read:

Places I need to visit

Index

Numbers

20 Books Vegas 41

A

Accuracy and Currency 54
ACES 46
Advertising 19, 20, 22, 132
Aliche, Tiffany 66
Angelou, Maya 90
Apple's Pages 61
Audience
   reading level 52
Audiobooks 13, 16, 92, 115
Author Brand 5, 20, 23, 85, 87, 89, 95, 97
   Build a community 108
Author platform 85, 89, 109
Autobiography 5, 32, 36

B

Baker & Taylor 75
Bayeza, Ifa 68
Best Platform Per Book Type 14
   Audiobooks 16
   E-books 15
   Print 14
Between the World and Me 65
Billion Dollar Lessons 65
Biography 35, 36, 39
Blogging 10, 21, 41, 88, 92, 93, 102, 107, 133, 134
BookBub 22
Book Covers 62, 63
   Abstract 63, 64
   Color Combinations 67
   Color Theory 65
   Font Styles 68
   Hiring Book Designers/
      Typesetters 69
   Illustrative 64
   Photographical 64
   Typographical 64
Book-Publishing Plan 5, 5
   Create a Book Budget 16
   Learning the Marketplace 8
   Narrowing Target Audience 7
   Path to Book Launch 19
   Set your Goals 6
   Timing is Everything 11
Bookshop.org 22
Bookstagrammers 41, 135
Booksy 22
Book trailers 17, 21
BookWright 61
Branding 20, 21, 23, 42, 68, 85-89, 93, 94, 97, 102, 104, 106, 109

corporate 85, 86
personal 85
Who are you 98
Bruised Hibiscus 66
Budget 16
Build courses 21
Butler, Octavia 90

C

Carroll, Paul B. 65
Chapman, Gary 31, 66
Characters 34
Character sketches 34
CIP (Cataloging in Publication) 74
Clarity 54
Clubhouse 19
Coaching 21, 109, 127
Coates, Ta-Nehisi 65
Copycats 91
Copyediting 13, 55, 132
Copy editors 45, 55, 82
Cover design
  Timeframe 13
Create Your Website 104
  About page 105
  call-to-action 105
  contact page 106
  Display your books 104
  reviews and endorsements 105
Creative nonfiction 36

D

Dark Girls 66
DBA (Doing Business As) 17, 18
Demographics 100
Designers 5, 61, 63, 69, 70, 128
Development of Fiction 34
Due, Tananarive 90
Duke, Bill 66
Dunbar, Erica Armstrong 66
Dyson, Michael Eric 66

E

E-books 15
Editing timeframes 12
Editorial Freelancers Association 46
Editorial Process 48, 49, 51
Editors 2, 9, 12, 37, 38, 41, 42, 45-50, 52, 55, 56, 58, 59, 74, 78, 82, 84, 125, 126, 135
  agreements 46
  copy editors. *See also* Copy Editors
  line editor 55, 125
  miscommunication 56
  questions to ask before hiring 46, 47
  relationship 45
  style guides 57
Editors of Color 46
Evaluating Publishing Houses 83

Index

Evaluating Similar Titles 9
Evans, Tony 66

F

Facebook 19, 21, 46, 73, 103, 107, 108, 133
Fill a void 8

G

Gates, Henry Louis Jr. 66
Gehry Partners 30
Get Good with Money 66
Ghostwriting
   Timeframe 13
Glymph, Jim 30
Goodreads 19, 22

H

Hooks, Bell 90

I

IBPA 41
Idea Mapping 26, 28, 29
   Journaling 28
   Transcripts and Presentations 29
InDesign 61, 129
Ingram 75, 130, 133
Innovative Interfaces 75
Instagram 19, 21, 41, 93, 107, 134, 135

Integrity 55
Intellectual property attorney 76, 77, 80
ISBN 2, 17, 74

J

John Wiley & Sons 76, 116
Jordan, June 90

K

Kincaid, Jamaica 65
King, Stephen 102

L

Layout design 61, 70, 133
Library of Congress Control Number (LCCN) 74, 75
LinkedIn 19, 21, 107
Literary agents 82
LLC (Limited Liability Company) 2, 17, 18, 74
Love 66

M

Marketing 10, 19, 134, 135
Memoir 5, 30, 32, 35, 36, 39, 54
Merchandise Branding 20
Morrison, Toni 66, 88, 90, 103, 106
Mosley, Walter 103

Mui, Chunka 65

N

Never Caught 66
Nunez, Elizabeth 66

O

Organization
  Concepts and Topics 53
  Depth 53
Our God is Awesome 66
Ownership of Content 75

P

Patreon 19
Permissions 45, 58, 77, 78, 127
Pinterest 19, 21, 41, 133, 135
Plot 35
P&L (Profit and Loss) estimate 82
Podcast 10, 19, 21, 22, 41, 88, 102, 107, 134, 135
Point of View/Narration 35
Powerful Prose Position (PPP) 100, 101, 103, 105, 109
Project management 58
  lack of 58
Publication Date 11
Publishers
  hybrid 83
  traditional 76, 80, 83, 84, 124
  Vanity presses 83

Publisher's Weekly 39, 42
Publishing attorney 76, 80
Publishing Contracts and Ownership 76
  Editing 78
  Grant of Rights 77
  Warranties and Reputations 77
Publishing method 13

R

Research 1, 8, 10, 13, 18, 22, 27, 33, 36, 37, 48, 49, 53, 55, 82, 91, 95, 126
Reviewers
  Beta reader 37-42, 58, 125
  Endorsers 37-42, 46, 133
  Peer Review 37, 39-42
Revising 29, 55
Revising Ideas 29
  Writing Various Versions 29
Ries, Al 97
Ries, Laura 97
Royalties 75, 79

S

Schedule 5, 11, 12, 58, 79, 82, 127, 135
Shange, Ntozake 68
Sing, Unburied, Sing 66
Social media 10, 17, 19-22, 46, 92, 93, 102-104, 106, 125, 134, 135

Index

Social media ads 10, 17, 21
Some Sing, Some Cry 68
Steele, Danielle 102
Story boards 34
Story objectives 34
Storytelling 35, 90
Subject Breakdown 26

T

Target Audience 5, 7, 8, 21, 27, 28, 33, 45, 47, 51, 99, 102, 108
The 22 Immutable Laws of Branding 97, 106, 116
The Autobiography of My Mother 65
The Color Purple 66
The Five Love Languages 31, 32, 66
The Signifying Money 66
The Underground Railroad 66
TikTok 19
Timeframe cover design 13
Timelines 34
Traditional and Templated Outline Models 26
Twitch 19, 21
Twitter 19, 107, 134, 135

U

US Copyright Office 74, 80

V

Vanity presses 83
Vellum 61
Virtual summit 21

W

Walker, Alice 66
Ward, Jesmyn 66
Whitehead, Colson 66
Writing plan
    one-year 36
Writing Style
    effectiveness 52

Y

YouTube 19, 21, 41, 104, 107, 134

www.ingramcontent.com/pod-product-compliance
Lightning Source LLC
Chambersburg PA
CBHW070044120526
44589CB00035B/2311